Why Do You
Believe What You
Believe About Jesus?

The Theological Foundations Series

Why Do You Believe What You Believe About Jesus?

Graham McFarlane

paternoster
press

First published in 2000 by Paternoster Press

06 05 04 03 02 01 00   7 6 5 4 3 2 1

Paternoster Press is an imprint of Paternoster Publishing,
P.O. Box 300, Carlisle, Cumbria, CA3 0QS, U.K.
and Paternoster Publishing, USA
PO Box 1047, Waynesboro, GA 30830-2047
http://www.paternoster-publishing.com

British Library Cataloguing in Publication Data
A catalogue record for this book is available from the British Library

ISBN 0-85364-958-8

Cover Design by Mainstream, Lancaster
Typeset by WestKey Ltd., Falmouth, Cornwall
Printed in Great Britain by Omnia Books Ltd., Glasgow

Contents

*In appreciation of all the students –
past and present – who have made the
teaching of Jesus Christ such a joy.*

1

Introduction

What do you believe about Jesus?

There is, possibly, no other person about whom you
could ask this question and expect *some* kind of
answer. Bar those who have never heard of him,
almost everyone has some sort of opinion about Jesus.
Almost no other person in the history of the human
race has exerted such influence as Jesus. His significance is all too noticeable. Think about it! Our calen-
dar year is determined by the relative timing of Jesus'
birth. Most of our holiday breaks have to do with
Jesus. A lot of cussing and swearing involves Jesus.
How we marry and bury are influenced in various
ways by the impact of Jesus. There is no getting away
from it. Jesus is a universally known figure.

IMPORTANT FACT

This is an important fact. We can say that Jesus is a
familiar figure world-wide. What we cannot say is that

what people know or think about Jesus is universally similar. We all buy into different versions of the story about Jesus. You may have your own story. It might be made up of different bits and pieces of information: conscious and unconscious. It may be rational or completely irrational. But it will be *your* story of Jesus.

Therefore, it makes sense to start by getting in touch with your version of the story. Why? Because the more important question concerns you, the reader. Just what *do* you believe about Jesus? Admittedly, you might think this is an odd question. Perhaps. But it is an important one.

Why?

Well, there are two reasons.

The **first** reason concerns you the reader. It is important for you to discover what you believe. After all, this is what you are bringing to the book. Your own prejudices or expectations will determine how you respond to what you read or hear. They will act as a conscious or subconscious yardstick. You may have it all worked out. Alternatively, you may be struggling to make sense of the subject. Or, you may not have a clue. Whatever the thoughts you have, believe it or not, what you think right now will influence how you read, understand, react to and engage with all that follows. This is an important point to take into account when writing on such an influential figure. Everyone, it would appear, has an opinion about Jesus, one way or another – whether they worship or reject him, are for him or against him.

Therefore, it makes sense right at the start to take time out, have a think and put pen to paper. Think of it as a consciousness-raising exercise. Put down what you believe about Jesus. A box is supplied below for the purpose. Nothing strenuous. Just what you could say in a couple of sentences. Then, you will have something to look back at when you get to the end of the book.

ACTIVITY

What I think about Jesus:

The **second** reason you need to know what you believe about Jesus concerns the subject matter in hand. It is the question Jesus posed to his first followers. In a nutshell, it is *the* question concerning Jesus. Mark puts it this way in his Gospel (8:27–29):

> Jesus and his disciples went on to the villages around Caesarea Philippi. On the way he asked them, "Who do people say I am?"
>
> They replied, "Some say John the Baptist; others say Elijah; and still others, one of the prophets."
>
> "But what about you?" he asked. "**Who do you say I am?**"
>
> Peter answered, "You are the Christ."

Here, the first followers of Jesus do exactly what you have just done. They are asked to identify what they believe about Jesus. Obviously, some of the meaning of their reply is lost on us today. We shall rectify this in subsequent chapters. What is important to note here, however, are three helpful aspects to their response.

- **There is something about Jesus that has made people ask questions and make assumptions.**

- **Jesus gets his followers to express impressions. He is drawing out the 'possiblies' and the 'probablies'.**

- **Jesus elicits a corporate and personal response from his disciples.**

The disciples, it would appear, are at a similar place to you. I can assume some kind of interest in Jesus on your part. Otherwise you would not be reading the book. There is obviously something about Jesus that merits interest.

Jesus asked his followers for their impressions. We have to admit that there are lots of different views going around about Jesus today. Baby Jesus; Bloodied Jesus; Divine Jesus; Best-friend Jesus; Loser Jesus; Crusading Jesus; Meet-all-my-needs Jesus; Historical Jesus; Gay Jesus; Anti-Gay Jesus; De-constructed Jesus; Fully God / Fully Human Jesus. Which one(s) is right?

Lastly, there has to be some kind of personal response to Jesus. It may be positive. Alternatively, it may be negative. Jesus' own dialogue, however, demands some kind of answer. For Peter it was decisive. Jesus is the Christ. But what kind of Christ? We shall look at this in detail later. What is important to note here, however, is that Peter's *what?* answer was fed by deeper *why?* reasons. That is, Peter's particular answer only made sense within a wider story. Like all good stories, the meaning grows as Jesus adds to Peter's response. It is an open-ended conversation which produces a counter-response from Jesus. However, ultimately, Jesus determines what it means to be "the Christ".

For the first disciples, however, one thing was clear. The question of Jesus' identity – of who Jesus *is* – is, itself, determined by what he *does*. After all, they saw him in action. So, it needs to be pointed out that initial beliefs about Jesus grew out of what he did as well as what he said. If you like, Jesus' words appear to have been backed up with action. It was because Jesus could *do* certain things that the first followers were forced to ask what kind of *person* was doing them! To this extent, then, the first followers of Jesus could do two things.

- **First**, they knew *what* they believed about Jesus. Peter probably speaks for them all. Jesus is the 'Christ', the Messiah.

- **Second**, as we have seen above, they knew *why* they believed what they believed about Jesus because they had seen Jesus in action. He *did* "Messiah" things.

Getting to know the story

Just gi'mme the facts!

In today's busy world, so many of us just want 'the facts'. But as we all know, facts mean nothing unless they are put in their right context. The spin doctors and advertising gurus can make facts mean whatever they want us to believe. And Christians are not so innocent either. With the rise of fundamentalism there is a great temptation just to go for the facts about Jesus as though they are magic, timeless truths. Of course, such aspirations belie a deeper unease concerning the conflict and confusion of our late and post-modern cultures. They reflect a desire for certainties in an uncertain world. And so we often project such needs onto Jesus. As long as we can run off a list of 'truths' about Jesus we feel safe. Admittedly, this works as long as we stay within the boundaries of similar thinking communities. It falls at the first hurdle, however, with the first, 'Why?'.

Why is this the case? It has to do with the fact that we forget that we no longer inhabit the same world as the first disciples of Jesus. What *they* believed about Jesus only made sense within the wider world in which they lived. Indeed, as we shall see, their belief was fed and transformed by this wider world. And so, there was some kind  of harmony between the two: between their belief about Jesus in particular and what the wider world around them thought, in general.

Unfortunately, this is not the case for today. What Christians believe is often not consonant with the wider worlds in which they live from day to day. Indeed, what many Christians believe has been

marginalized to the private and individual compart-
ments of those worlds they inhabit. For most of the
twentieth century, Christian belief has been very much
a private affair. Over time, the *whats?* and the *whys?*
have become separated. The end result is that it is now
possible to find Christians today who know *what* they
believe about Jesus but cannot give any credible
answer to the deeper reasons for holding such beliefs.
In short, they do not know *why* they believe what they
believe. Consequently, they have no meaningful
answers to offer those asking today's questions.

This is a dangerous place to be! If we are to resolve the
present situation, two changes of mind have to happen.

> **We need to rediscover the world of
> the first Christians.**

What we have to do is to rediscover the way in which
the first followers of Jesus understood their world. We
need to do this because, as we have seen, it was this
wider world of belief and expectation that informed
their *particular* understanding of Jesus.

If you think about it,
this is just plain, com-
mon sense. Perhaps I
can illustrate it by giv-
ing a personal example.
When I was a teenager I
had a penfriend in Italy.

We wrote for over five years before I was able to visit her. Over those years we got to know each other fairly well. Yet it was not until I visited her world, her family, her friends that I really got to know her. As a result, when I wrote after that visit I was able to locate her within a wider world. I remembered the aromas and the food, I understood the culture, I even recollected accents and gestures. In essence, I read her stories *in situ*. It was now easier to understand my friend. It was also harder to misunderstand her.

So with Jesus. Without a prior understanding of his world and the expectations of those who followed him it is easy to read the stories wrongly. The history of New Testament studies only goes to prove that point. All too easily we project our presuppositions onto Jesus. He becomes the Jesus we expect to find. As a result we muffle the story and turn Jesus into a muted and domesticated version of our own desires and expectations.

> **We need to inhabit the stories and become familiar with their world.**

In turn, we can retell them for each new generation for each new world. We have to do this because our worlds never stand still: we are constantly changing. We change as individuals. We also change as communities, nations and cultures.

- *Communities* tend to be firmly rooted in some kind of identity that gives them a particular shape and colour.

- *Nations* hold onto collective identities.

- *Culture* is constantly adapting and thus constantly moving. Being more fluid in its boundaries, it is more difficult to define.

EVIDENCE?

Take fashion, for instance. Fashion is an expression of what people believe. In the sixties it was bold and colourful because the world was seen in those terms. In the thirties, it was grey and dull, because there was little to be bright about. This tells us something important about the way the world around us operates. It is this. Much of our collective activity is dominated by what we believe to be important. And what we deem important is dominated at a more subconscious level by what we hope for. We gather this all up in our *cultural activities*. We see it in our grand buildings: they are declarations of hope and pride in our abilities. What are the  impressive and spectacular ones today? They are not churches: religion is not the future. Neither are they schools and universities: learning is not the future. Nor are they hospitals: charity is not the future. Rather, they are the finance centres. These impressive buildings of commerce and finance tell us, at a much more basic level, that our hope is in this area. Money is the future – for the moment. However, in time this centre of salvation will recede. Another will take its place. Water will be the future. Or perhaps oil. Or space travel away from an increasingly self-polluting world...

THE POINT IS THIS:

our centres of hope are constantly changing. Therefore, if Christians are to reclaim some of that ground two things have to happen. **On the one hand,** there is the need to be able to say something about who is on offer – Jesus. This involves the *what?* and *why?* dimensions concerning Jesus. **On the other hand,** there is the need to be able to address these Jesus-dimensions to the issues of our own day-to-day worlds. This involves being *culturally* aware. As the culture moves – so must we. As Graham Cray comments: the recipients of our message are constantly changing address.

Our task, then, is twofold:

• to discover the new address

• to deliver the message in user-friendly terms which do not undermine the content of our message.

This is the challenge facing us today – unless we want to be left behind as dinosaurs!

The purpose of the book

At the heart of this book
lie two levels of inquiry.
On the one hand, we can
discover *what* Christians
believe about Jesus. This is exciting but not always as
straightforward as we think. Belief, any belief, about
the ultimate meaning of life is likely to require some
hard work. **On the other hand**, we have the chance to
dig deeper. We can discover *why* Christians hold such
beliefs. This is the more demanding part of the book.
It involves additional spade-work. It involves some
personal reflection, too. In order to aid you in this
there will be various activities to which you the reader
can apply yourself. Hopefully, they will help you along
the way.

But be encouraged! Much of what is in this book has
been taught to several different groups of students. So
far, most of them, if not all, have enjoyed the course!
Our task is also an exciting one. Why? Because once
you can identify what you believe about Jesus and go
on to explain in helpful terms why you believe such
things – then you are equipped for service. You will be
able to field all sorts of questions, engage with all types
of people and enter into all kinds of situations. In each
and in all, you will be able to become 'a worker who
does not need to be ashamed and who correctly
handles the word of truth', (2 Tim. 2:15).

The
New
Testament
Stories
of
Jesus

2

Making Sense of Jesus

No doubt you will be familiar with the saying, 'Have your cake and eat it too'. It denotes a particular attitude. It usually corresponds to a situation in which there are two conflicting motives, ideas or directions.

 Both are important, necessary, desirable. And we want both. We all find ourselves in such positions from time to time. There is a particularly *religious* version that crops up in relation to what some people think about Jesus. It, too, involves two conflicting desires. On the one hand, there is the desire to make Jesus central to what we believe. On the other hand, there is the desire to be relevant to the world around us. These are real tensions and they lie at the very heart of Christian faith. The good news is that they *can* be resolved – usually by much hard work.

However, there are **two** unhelpful responses and they fall into the category of wanting to have one's cake and eat it too! Each response is very much alive and kicking today. Each needs to be resisted if we are to say in any credible way *why* we believe *what* we believe about Jesus.

The **FIRST** response gets round the tension by being so heavenly-minded about Jesus that the answer is of no earthly use! Here, God becomes so *transcendent* that there are no points of contact with the day-to-day world of ordinary people. God is understood to be remote, distant and very different from us. It follows, then, that if Jesus is understood to be totally divine his humanity tends to get absorbed in his 'godness'. As a result, the human story of Jesus usually gets lost in amongst the divine story. This is rarely deliberate. Rather, it is merely the consequence of what happens when the human-side-of-the-story is neglected. In addition, when this happens it usually means that the story of Jesus gets stuck in the past. It very rarely has any significant meaning for today. It tends to get 'hidden' in a sacred past that has very little to do with today.

This approach suffers from over-emphasizing the story of Jesus at the expense of its meaning and relevance for today.

This first response tends to be found more in conservative circles and is becoming increasingly the hallmark of fundamentalist religion. It is the private story of an increasingly withdrawing religious subculture. That is, it belongs to those groups of people who do not seek any dialogue with the worlds around them. Security

for them is found in 'not engaging' with the outside world. As a result, their message may well make sense inside the camp. However, it very rarely makes contact with those most in need of its life-giving answers. The end results are clusters of 'holy huddles' scattered around the country unaware that they are completely irrelevant.

The tension here, then, is resolved by letting go of the world and holding onto the story. Consequently, the story of Jesus may well be faithfully preserved – it is static – at worse – dead. However, it is not getting out to its intended audience. After all, Jesus announced that he came not to heal the healthy but those who are sick (Luke 5:31–32). What needs to be added, therefore, to this response is engagement with real people, real questions, real life.

The **SECOND** response is the opposite of the first. It tends to be so earthly-minded that it is of no heavenly use! Rather than being too transcendent, this approach is too *immanent*. That is, it is too rooted in the here and now to make any sense of another, different, alternative way of seeing, doing and responding. Here, the story of Jesus is placed under the more pressing needs of the different worlds to which we belong. Unlike the first response, this one usually maintains a very healthy engagement with these different worlds. What is not so healthy, however, is the fact that this activity tends to take place at the expense of the story of Jesus. Or, rather, it tends to take place at the expense of the world within which the story of Jesus makes sense. Underlying this approach is a false assumption. It is this.

The stories about Jesus belong to a primitive world. It was less enlightened, less scientific, less reliable than ours today. We need to take this into account before accepting what these stories say. They cannot talk into our own worlds without radical translation and revision. Obviously, if the original writers had known what we know today they would have said things differently. We need, therefore, to *reinterpret* the story of Jesus so that it makes sense of what we know today.

Whilst this is a laudable task, this approach brings with it a significant danger. It is this. **It usually occurs at the expense of the original story.** Jesus becomes so similar to us that there is little reason for making him the central focus of one's faith. Nine times out of ten we end up simply looking at our own cultural reflection. Jesus is made in our own image. There is little point, then, in switching allegiance as a response to the questions that are being asked. One response merely apes the other.

> **Rather, something more dynamic has to happen. The world of Jesus and the stories about it need to be recaptured and brought back to life.**

Each of these different responses demands proper consideration. Each is valid to some degree or another.

Each contains a great element of truth. It is simply not necessary to pillory one against the other. Nor does it reflect the essential character of the story of Jesus to play one off in order to elevate the other. One helpful way to overcome the impasse is to see that the problem is more to do with what is *not* being said rather than what is. Thus each needs to be balanced by incorporating what is missing from it, what it is not saying and doing. For this to happen, we may need to listen again to and respect the different stories of Jesus. To do this will mean entering into their worlds and letting *them* address *us*.

One thing, though, needs to be pointed out. This procedure will only take us back to the original and inevitable tension involved in stating *why* we believe *what* we believe about Jesus. It will not resolve it! For this resolution to happen, a lot more hard work needs to take place.

Telling our stories

The good news is that it is possible for our stories to interact with the original stories of Jesus. In the past, scholars have made the task difficult with their own belief about the inaccessibility of the biblical world. However, a new consensus is emerging. This coincides with a wider cultural turn. One major expression of this turn away from modernity is in the way we perceive the past and its stories. Increasingly, scholars are beginning to argue that storytelling is a universal and human activity. We *all* describe our world through the stories we tell. Additionally, scholars are beginning to admit that the historical scepticism of the past is not altogether warranted. Perhaps history does have something to tell us. More, it is possible to access the past through the stories it hands on to  us. And they do not need to be 'neutral' or uncontaminated by someone else's perspective. After all, every recollection, every report, every event is told from the perspective of the one telling, reporting, writing. There is, it would appear, no such thing as 'timeless' truth within time and history.

Consequently, it is no longer acceptable to dismiss the past simply because it is 'the past'. There is no cash value in dismissing out of hand the stories of earlier generations. As George Lindbeck points out, such stories constitute the very *grammar* of faith. They did so for the first Christians and continue to do so today. As he puts it,

> **'It was the scriptural text that structured their cosmos, their communities and their self-descriptions as saints and sinners, saved or damned.'**
>
> 'Atonement and the Hermeneutics of Intratextual Social Embodiment' in *The Nature of Confession* (eds. T.R. Phillips, D.L. Okholm; Downers Grove, IL: IVP, 1996), p. 226

It was the biblical stories that moulded how the first believers understood and lived in their worlds. The task today demands that we apply the same double agenda. We need *first* to recover these same biblical stories and discover what they are trying to tell us. But *secondly* we need to understand our own stories and how we see things today. When we do this, we discover some interesting differences.

For instance, have you noticed something about the present climate of thought? Our hope in the future appears to be waning. Increasingly we live for the

present. A good example of this is the collapse of the things we have come to think as unshakeable: the financial markets.

The prospect of ongoing profiteering is increasingly coming under scrutiny and doubt. So our confidence in the future shifts. This has, in turn, a knock-on effect concerning how we perceive ourselves. It means that we do not necessarily view the 'past' as the opposite of the 'future'. Rather, we recognize that the past may have something to tell us about the present.

This, in turn, enables us to meet each other more realistically. We take it for granted that there are different views on the same issue. We are all coming from different places, each with its own different *story*. That is a fact of life. And if you really think about it, it has always been like this. The issue is more to do with how we handle such differences. Paul's experience at the Areopagus (Acts 17:22–23) shows how such differences can be handled.

> Paul then stood up in the meeting of the Areopagus and said: 'People of Athens! I see that in every way you are very religious. For as I walked around and looked carefully at your objects of worship, I even found an altar with this inscription: TO AN UNKNOWN GOD. Now what you worship as something unknown I am going to proclaim to you.

Then, as now, there was a rich assortment of beliefs on offer. At the same time, we are now no longer willing to be gagged by one view. As the Establishment story, whether secular or religious, wanes, so alternative voices can be heard. There is a whole market of stories out there and each one presumes the right to be heard. In a market economy even our stories have to be tendered. Yet, it is not the plethora of stories that is the issue. No! There always have been competing stories – always will be. The rubber hits the road at the point of *significance* and *meaning*.

> The issue is not
>
> **WHAT**
>
> story do you believe,
>
> but
>
> **DOES YOUR STORY MAKE**
>
> **SENSE?**

Can you see what is at stake here?

In order to answer this issue meaningfully we have both to know the original stories of Jesus (what we believe) *and* be able to communicate them for today (making sense). This is simply what Paul does at the Areopagus. He is able to do so because he both knows and understands what he believes about Jesus. Consequently, he can tell others.

Asking questions

The aim of this book is to help make this happen! I
have been encouraged in believing that this is not only
possible but can even be **enjoyable**. The evidence defies
refute! I have seen this happen both in the college lec-
ture and in the church sermon, in the auditorium and

in a cafe. After ten years of teaching about Jesus at London Bible
College I am convinced that
people really do want to engage
at both levels of thought. They
want to know the answers to the
what? as well the *why?* questions
about Jesus. I have seen students
get excited about who Jesus is as
they begin to engage with the

original questions and enter the world of the first
followers of Jesus. In turn, I have seen this activity
transform private and individual faith into something
that wants to go out and engage with others. It may be
over a meal, it may be on the doorstep with the local
Jehovah's Witnesses. It may be in the pub, the kitchen,
the church foyer, the gym. It *is* possible and it can be
very enjoyable.

In addition, I have been encouraged throughout this
time by the cultural changes going on as I have struggled to make sense of what I believe. This really is a
good time to be a thinking Christian. In terms of how
we can go about this, I hold firmly to the belief that in
order to understand Jesus as his closest disciples did we

must enter into the questions they asked. In *their* dialogue with Jesus they arrived at their answers. These answers made sense of Jesus. Admittedly, they never fully resolved the tensions. But at least they helped in making sense of this remarkable person. Consequently, I have been driven by the belief that unless we enter into the world of their questions we shall not discover the real Jesus. In turn, unless we enter into the world of questions subsequent Christians have asked and engage with the answers they provide, we shall be unable to answer our own questions. The aim, ultimately, in all of this is to be able to give our own personal and corporate responses to this central question:

?

Why

Do

I

Believe

What

I

Believe

About

Jesus

?

What we are going to do, then, is enter this world of belief. This will involve going back to the New Testament. This is the gist of the book. Hopefully, we shall see that the New Testament does not have **one single** view on Jesus. This is surprising to many people. Rather, it contains a **number** of perspectives on Jesus. Each seeks to make sense of a particular side to Jesus and his work. Maybe lights are going on already as you begin to realize that our task involves building up a 3-D picture. A bit like a constellation, the New Testament offers various windows of belief and perspective until a bigger, wider, more meaningful picture emerges.

In doing so we engage in an ancient activity. It is what Christians have been doing since the very genesis of their faith. In Latin it is called *fides quaerens intellectum* – **faith seeking understanding**. As the first Christians came to believe in Jesus so they sought to make sense of that faith. No 'blind faith' here, no 'just believe'. This is radical and fully thoughtful. We must hold onto the audacity of the first Christians and the stories they told in order to make sense of Jesus. Our task is not really very different. Any kind of belief demands explanation – unless it is completely irrational! And we should reflect the same audacity as we confront today's stories with the story of Jesus.

We turn, then, and seek to discover Jesus through the world of his first followers. This will involve finding out what they thought about him, how they made sense of him, and why they followed him.

3

Accessing the Past:
The Original Context

The task of proper Christian God-talk – what we call *theology* – is to express and describe what we believe about God and Jesus Christ. To do this,

 Christians must look for the broader picture, especially when the subject is Jesus. This means that we need to know what we are dealing with. Our first task, then, has to involve going back into the original world of the first Christians. We need to let the original text speak to us. Once we do this we discover the context within which their words first made sense. This will, inevitably, mean that we go back to a different time, to different horizons, to different histories. This is important. Seldom do we realize that our perception of how things were can be

no more than an imposing of our world onto the past. The best example of this is to be seen in the way baby Jesus has been painted down through the centuries. A walk though the Sainsbury's Wing at London's National Gallery provides the proof. Again and again, Jesus is a white, Anglo-Saxon, blue-eyed, western male. He is painted in **our** image.

This is the downside of the challenge.

The upside is that once we make contact with the world of the first Christians we can hear better their thoughts, understand more clearly their questions and appreciate more fully their answers. In turn, we shall grasp the brilliance of their solutions and understand why they have come to take on an authority that still enlightens us today. In short, their story will impact ours with an unlimited range of possibilities.

Asking the right questions

In order to ask the right questions about Jesus we need to delve into the older, Jewish stories. As we do so we encounter a world of expectation and hope that was as old as the Jewish Bible itself. This serves as the horizon against which the Christian faith emerged. In turn, we unlock and discover the truer meanings to the stories told by the first Christians as they sought to make sense of Jesus.

We saw earlier that Christian faith, indeed any living faith, is all about two things: understanding of oneself and understanding of what one encounters beyond onself. It is **faith seeking understanding**. And as with all such endeavours, it involves asking questions.

Therefore, we should not be surprised that the same principle applies when we explore our beliefs about Jesus. The ability to offer meaningful answers demands first of all that we ask the right questions and think about them. If you think about it, this is only com-

mon sense. The scientist resolves a problem by asking the correct questions. The doctor identifies the medical problem by putting the right questions to the patient.

> **The Christian discovers the proper story of Jesus by asking the questions needed in order to unlock the narrative.**

This is faith seeking understanding. This is Christian theology.

What Christians believe about Jesus does not – never will – grow out of nothing. Belief is the answer to questions that have been asked and answered well.

Jesus is the Answer!

What is the question?

Something about Jesus demanded an answer *then* and continues to demand one *now*. As we shall see, much of the *what-we-believe-about-Jesus* is simply the answer to these primary questions.

Two contemporary Christian thinkers help us here. The first is Schubert Ogden. He has identified two 'tracks' for our understanding of Jesus: for our christology. The first track he calls a **christology of witness**. By this Ogden means that what we believe about Jesus should relate to what actually happened. John, perhaps, best represents the first Christians and their christologies of witness, in the opening verses of his first letter (1 Jn. 1:1–3).

That which was from the beginning, which we have heard, which we have seen with our eyes, which we have looked at and our hands have touched – this we proclaim concerning the Word of life. The life appeared; we have seen it and testify to it, and we proclaim to you the eternal life, which was with the Father and has appeared to us. We proclaim to you what we have seen and heard, so that you also may have fellowship with us.

This is eye-witness theology. It is the 'what' of what we believe. It is faith thinking and speaking. It is giving words to what has been seen and heard.

The second track is a different type of thinking. This is a **christology of reflection**. This is the 'why' dimension. Such reflection consists of more than factual witness. It involves an interpretative process. It concerns the meaning of both what has happened (the event) and how it impacts the reader or listener (the context). The story, then, consists of two distinctions:

• On the one hand there is Jesus in himself.

• On the other, there is Jesus and his meaning for us.

In the recent past it was trendy to say that these two distinctions did not necessarily need to be the same. Ogden, for instance, argued that we could only accept what seemed **appropriate** and **credible**. However, in doing so, the horizon of the reader is being imposed too heavily upon the original witness. After all, the above witness of John appears to be fully aware that witness and reflection go hand in hand. More recent debate favours an alternative approach that insists that we must allow *our* world to be addressed, challenged and changed by that of the text. We must allow the world of *Jesus* to impact *our* world.

This is where our second Christian thinker, Tom Wright, comes in. He identifies questions that have to be asked in the task of telling the Christian story. He locates such questions within the wider context of **world-view**. Since this is an important factor in any telling of the Jesus story, it may be helpful to look  at what is meant by the term, 'world-view'. Wright identifies a world-view by the following four criteria:

- **World-views provide the stories with which we understand reality.**

- **These world-view-stories enable us to answer the basic questions of human existence.**

- **We express our answers to such questions through cultural symbols.**

- **Our world-view provides ways of living in the world.**

N.T. Wright, *The New Testament and the People of God* (London: SPCK, 1993), pp. 123–4.

It would appear, then, that we can no more do without a world-view than we can a mouth, our lungs, our heart. It is the invisible framework within which we make sense of ourselves. As such, it is necessary for any credible story about Jesus. Jesus only has significance to the degree he actually addresses the problems of his day. In order to do this, we need to ask some basic questions:

1) **Who are we?**

2) **Where are we?**

3) **What is wrong?**

4) **What is the solution?**

These appear to be rather simple questions, but it may be a good exercise at this point to answer these questions for yourself. They are some of the most significant windows into how you view reality. If nothing else it will show where the missing parts are in your own story about Jesus.

ACTIVITY

Look at the above questions and give your own answer to each of them.

1)

2)

3)

4)

If the world of the first Christian witnesses is to impact ours seriously then we need to attend to the more specific questions of their own story. Wright identifies **six** questions that are helpful in unlocking the *world-view* of the first Christians. They serve as the invisible background to everything that is said about Jesus. If we can get their answers to such questions, then we are in a better position to understand what is being said about Jesus. They are as follows:

- **How did Jesus fit into Judaism?**

- **What were Jesus' aims?**

- **Why did Jesus die?**

- **How and why did the early church begin?**

- **Why are the Gospels what they are?**

- **How does the Jesus we discover by doing 'history' relate to the contemporary church and world?**

N.T. Wright, *Jesus and the Victory of God* (London: SPCK, 1996), pp. 89–117.

These world-view questions serve as doors into the world of the first Christian writers and thinkers. Without them we fail to read what is being really said. We miss the signals that would be so familiar to the first readers. It would be like being at a dinner party with a blindfold on. You would be able to hear what was being said but you would not know how it was being said. Without the body language, the words would be less meaningful. Similarly, without the understanding that such broad questions provide we fail to ask the right questions. In doing so we fail to discover the full meaning and impact of the original answers.

What are the specific questions that need to be asked  about the particular world of Jesus? We need to understand that the story of Jesus only makes sense against the wider story of Judaism and the Hebrew Bible. Both serve as the backdrop for the drama of Jesus. Both constitute the *world-view* of the first Christians.

Without such an understanding we all too easily read our own interpretation of things onto Jesus and the faith of the first witnesses.

Perhaps at this stage it may be helpful to merge the different sets of questions that we have been looking at. This will enable us to arrive at a broader set of world-view questions. With them we will be better able to engage with the world of Jesus and his first followers. A helpful way of putting them may be as follows:

Who is God?

Who is Jesus?

Where are we?

Who are we?

What is wrong?

What is the solution?

The task, then, is to go back to the world-view from which Jesus and his story emerge. From this, we shall begin to make sense of the different ways in which the first witnesses talk about Jesus. This will involve engagement with all the questions stated above, both directly and indirectly. In essence, it will involve walking into the world of Jesus. It necessitates a knowledge of the Jewish story.

The Jewish story

Perhaps this is a good place to stop and do some personal reflection. The following exercise will no doubt be easy for some – difficult for others.

ACTIVITY

Write down 10 things you know about the world in which Jesus lived:

1)

2)

3)

4)

5)

6)

7)

8)

9)

10)

Hopefully, this exercise will enable you to see how much or how little you really know. Either way, it serves as a consciousness-raising exercise. It helps locate us into another world: a world very different from our own. This is very important when it comes to finding out about the real Jesus.

WHY?

There is a kind of cultural arrogance that presumes that the foreigner thinks just like us. It is a universal problem. In short, we automatically presume that our way is the norm and therefore the only way of doing things. Anyone who has made any attempts at cross-cultural communication or mission will know, however, that this is not the case. We all see the world through our own cultural windows. We all see through culturally-tinted glasses, to some degree or other. Only the most empathic and sensitive of people appear not to succumb to this kind of assumption.

Translate this assumption, then, into our view of the world of the Bible, and serious malfunctions begin to occur. By imposing our world onto the world of the Bible we fail to understand its *otherness*. If we assume that the first Christians thought like us today, we tend to fall prey to the kind of arrogance mentioned above. Rather, we need to allow the  world-views of the Jewish and Christian Bibles to speak to us. When this happens we discover a world-view very different from our own. In turn, we begin to access the hope and expectation that fuelled the faith of the first-century believer.

In doing so, we discover two things.

FIRSTLY, we discover a world of expectation and hope that was both *already there* as well as one in the process of *evolving*. If we are to understand the Jesus of this world we need to access the *already*. That is, we need to know enough about the ins and outs of this world so that we can read between the lines of what is said. This is common sense. Think about it: we never mention the obvious when we speak to our closest friends. We take it for granted. It is part of our world-view. As such we *speak into* a world of presupposi-tions. Our handicap as readers from another culture and century, then, is that we do not know this world-view. We do not operate out of this knowledge. We operate from our own. Consequently, we miss many of the things that were obvious to the first readers and hearers. It takes time and serious study to see out of a world-view different from your own. However, it is important if we are to discover the common-sense beliefs of the day.

SECONDLY, once we know what was commonly believed around the time of Jesus we can see if what the first Christians believed was different. And if it was different we can see just how and where. When this happens, we can then ask . . .

. . . *Why?*

4

Are You the Christ?

When John heard in prison what Christ was doing, he sent his disciples to ask him, "Are you the one who was to come, or should we expect someone else?"

Jesus replied, "Go back and report to John what you hear and see: The blind receive sight, the lame walk, those who have leprosy are cured, the deaf hear, the dead are raised, and the good news is preached to the poor. Blessed is anyone who does not fall away on account of me."

(Matt. 11:2–6)

Why was John so concerned about getting Jesus' identity right? Why was it such an issue that from prison he went to the trouble of sending his followers to ask such a blunt question? It must have been very important for him.

We can surmise that behind the question asked by John of Jesus are at least two expectations. **Firstly,** there was a profound sense of longing. John will no  doubt have been raised with a sense of destiny. His own conception and birth, after all, were the things tales are made of. Ageing parents, angelic visitations and a bizarre birth (Luke 1:39–80) will have set the foundations for a strong sense of identity and destiny. He had to find out. Too much was at stake.

Secondly, however, beyond the personal agenda lay a more national expectation. For centuries the Jewish people had held onto the hope that one day their God would deliver them. This was, originally, a *collective* and *national* hope: something that pertained to the nation as a whole. The *entire* nation would share in this hope and experience its reality. In turn, this hope would be realized *nationally* through a *particular* figure, someone who would save them from their enemies. This person was the Messiah, or, in Greek, the Christ.

The Messiah, the hope of Israel and Jesus

This, then, was the hope of Israel. And it was a strong one. Its roots went far back into their national and religious identity. It was fed by the belief that one day the

Lord God would restore the fortunes of Israel. Such an event would take place through the nation in general and through the agency of his chosen leader, the anointed one, the Messiah, in particular.

Thus, an entire nation, generations of the faithful, gathered their hopes in this future restoration. This was a restoration not in the sweet by and by, but very much rooted in time, in a particular place, for a particular people. It would be a very here-and-now event. We have to remember that by the time of Jesus the Jewish nation had undergone a progressive fall in fortunes. In prior history Israel had been a powerful nation under its most illustrious king, King David (around 1000 BC). Things began to go wrong under his son, Solomon. By around 926 BC the two kingdoms of Israel and Judah divided under Jeroboam I (Israel) and Rehoboam (Judah). By around 526 BC the kingdom of Israel was no more. In turn, Judah underwent several occupations.

The people were scattered. Their hope was diluted. Yet it persisted. As things got worse, so the hope was strengthened. One day, the Lord God would rise up on their behalf and rescue them. He had to! It was this God who had created everything that exists. Moreover, this

God had made an agreement – a covenant – with them that could no more be broken than the cosmos disintegrate. Therefore the promise of reinstatement, of national elevation, *had to* happen one day.

Their God, then, would rescue them, restore them, make good the desolation, despair and depression they had long experienced. Ruling nation after nation oppressed them, but still the hope remained. Perhaps by the same method that rumours spread, or through their religious consciousness, a national and collective hope emerged that was located in one particular figure or group. This figure or group would be their saviour. The evidence would be seen in what was done. And what was achieved would happen by virtue of being empowered by the very Spirit of God. There had to be the Spirit's anointing. As such, this individual or collective group would be the 'Anointed One': the Messiah in Hebrew, in Greek, the 'Christ'. Through the empowering of God's Spirit the messianic figure or group would restore the fortunes of the chosen people.

The Gospel texts do not speak of or narrate this hope. They do not need to. It is part of the underlying world-view of the different authors. Enough is given by both Matthew and Luke for us to know that John the Baptist also held this world-view: he shared in it. However, he had to know. That he sent others to inquire after his cousin suggests that his own expectation did not quite correlate with what he was hearing and seeing. Had he got it wrong? Should he be looking for someone else? Has he been announcing the wrong person? Is there someone else?

What kind of Messiah?

It is of interest to note, then, how Jesus replies. There is no, 'Tell John I am the long-awaited Messiah'. There is no speaking into an established set of criteria. They did not really exist. The concept of Messiah was, to put it bluntly, a fluid one. Neither, however, is there any negative reply. Jesus, whatever he says, does not close the conversation. Rather, what we have is an indirect reply. What is of interest is the fact that in giving *this* reply Jesus gives John not only an answer to the question but also a redefinition of what he is looking for.

Jesus replies with words that lay at the very heart of Jewish expectation. In giving his answer, Jesus is saying, 'Look at what I do then match it with the right person'. In typically Jewish form, Jesus invites his inquirers to engage in a very practical test. Look at the facts. Let them announce what really is going on. Lest John's disciples are slow on the uptake, Jesus gives this prompter. He cites a very particular passage from the book of Isaiah. The big give-away, here, is that in going to *this* text, Jesus lets us know exactly what lay behind his act. It revealed the *motivation* that would lie behind every subsequent act. This passage reveals to us his declaration of intent. It is his manifesto.

> The Spirit of the Sovereign LORD is
>   on me,
> because the LORD has anointed me
>   to preach good news to the poor.
> He has sent me to bind up the
>   broken-hearted,
>   to proclaim freedom for the
>   captives
>   and release from darkness for the
>   prisoners,
> to proclaim the year of the LORD's
>   favour
>   and the day of vengeance of our
>   God,
> to comfort all who mourn.
> (Isa. 61:1–2)

Here, then, is one of the most penetrating insights into Jesus' own self-identity. This is a declaration of intent. It is the way Jesus identifies himself.

But what is Jesus saying?

How can we be sure of what Jesus meant when he talked about his own identity or calling? Traditionally, scholars have trawled literature around the time of Jesus in order to find parallels. Once a similar saying or use of a saying is discovered or identified, similarities and differences can be assessed. Theories are devised, counter-theories are developed, and so forth. Some are helpful, others are not. Some stand the test of time, others go. From the good ones we are able to establish two things. On the one hand we discover what people thought around the time of Jesus. On the other hand, we see how different Jesus' thoughts were from the thoughts of those around him. Perhaps no more so than with the concept of Messiah.

We have to allow for two tracks of thought. **Firstly**, the identity and role of the Messiah were open-ended.  There were no fixed criteria for identifying the Messiah. Indeed, there were a few different messianic figures to choose from. He would be a royal figure, a descendent of King David. Such a person could lay claim to very strong biblical foundations (Ps. 2; 18; 20; 21; 45; 72; 89; 110; 132). Nationalism and imperialism inevitably merge together in such a figure. Victory over national aggressors was a natural step in thought. Needless to say, heirs to the royal title could have easily entertained valid messianic aspirations. By and large, *messiah* and *king* were closely aligned.

Additionally, there is evidence to suggest that around the time of Jesus there was also expectation of a non-royal messianic figure. This messianic figure was more *priestly* than royal, an interpreter of the Law, and does not appear to be seen in conflict with its royal counterpart.

Secondly, however, we must allow for Jesus having his own unique and original understanding of the concept of the Messiah. We can  discover if this is so by asking whether Jesus understood himself in any of the more traditional ways. The passage Jesus cites to John's followers gives us a clue. The first point to be made is this. Jesus replies by giving John's followers descriptions of the kingdom of God. Or, to put it differently, Jesus describes himself as doing the kind of things that should be happening if God is at work. If these things are happening then God's agenda, rule, way of doing things – God's kingdom – is in operation. Anyone seriously interested in locating where God is at work would expect to see these things taking place.

The kingdom of God only operates if God is at work.

However, we cannot let things stay here. We need to locate Jesus' agenda within the wider horizon of Judaism. Only against this backdrop will his own aims and objectives make sense. In a nutshell, Jesus has a mission. It has to do with **liber-ation**. Matthew has already identified this to be the case in Jesus' reply to John's followers. Luke goes a step further in retelling the first public act of Jesus after his forty-day ordeal in the desert. Jesus claims the words of Isaiah 61:1–2 and then announces (Luke 4:21):

> **TODAY THIS SCRIPTURE IS FULFILLED IN YOUR HEARING.**

In one stroke, Jesus does two things.

- He identifies his mission in very well-known biblical terms – the *freedom* promised in Isaiah.

- He personally claims this high point of Old Testament promise to apply to himself.

What kind of freedom?

But note: the Messiah's identity is inextricably tied up with the wider hope of freedom. Of course, it goes without saying that the notion of *freedom* was at the top of the agenda for the contemporary Jew at the time of Jesus. The messianic hope had everything to do with *freedom*. This is neither unique nor original. What *is* so original is the fact that Jesus *both* absorbs it into his own agenda and mission *and* then redefines it.

WHY?

Only a free nation and society can be victorious. It went almost without saying: the messianic figure would be an agent of liberation, of freedom. Through the Messiah God's ultimate agenda would be realized. We catch a glimpse of this deep hope in the words of Jesus' followers immediately after his death (Luke 24:19–21). When recounting their own personal hopes they said of Jesus.

> He was a prophet, powerful in word and deed before God and all the people. The chief priests and our rulers handed him over to be sentenced to death, and they crucified him;
> *but we had hoped that he was the one who was going to redeem Israel.*

Judaism at the time of Jesus understood this in purely nationalistic-religious terms. It would appear that even those closest to Jesus were not free from such expectation. Perhaps even in their minds was the thought that the Romans would be ousted and true national and religious freedom would occur.

However, this is not what Jesus thought. The solution turns on identifying one or two definitions. For instance, did this kind of nationalistic fervour reflect the aims of God's covenant with his chosen people, the descendants of Abraham? Or was it purely wishful – albeit political – thinking? The place of the true Messiah, the true Christ, will only become clear once this is answered.

Alternatively, does the freedom that God promised his people necessarily have to be expressed in such nationalistic and religious terms? True, it is impossible for a group of people, especially the Jewish people, not to express their freedom in both national and religious ways. Yet, this freedom only makes sense against a more aristocratic story. It is the story that defines the Jewish believer. It is a story of promise, of exile, of hope. It is one of promise made to Abraham, encoded  in the Torah, enshrined in the Temple, embodied in the long-awaited Messiah. This much Jesus and his followers will have believed. It was their common worldview encapsulated in the symbols of liberation annually celebrated at Passover and the Day of Atonement. The uniqueness and originality of Jesus and the early Christian stories is that all this comes to fulfilment in Jesus. This is radical. This is original. And for the Jewish believers of the day, it was scandalous –

as it is for us today. Yet for the first Christian believers, it was good news. It represented the fulfilment of all their hopes. It offered them the freedom they had as a nation collectively hoped for.

WHAT SORT OF FREEDOM?

The question, however, begs to be asked. Just what kind of freedom are we talking about here? After all, there are many different liberation-expressions. There is the freedom to take up arms. Or the freedom of speech, to express oneself. What kind of freedom is Jesus into?

It is the freedom promised by God to his covenant people and through them to the entire world.

It is a liberation from all that oppresses and destroys. It focuses on the marginalized and the rejected.

Economically, it is radically different from state or Temple economies. It is not possible to give allegiance to both *and* participate in this freedom. The one mitigates against the other. The State and Temple are subtle forms of bondage where people

are rewarded and punished by unfair standards. Jesus' new freedom is a radical expression of freedom and liberation where people are released from being commodities. Freedom takes on a relational face.

Politically, it challenges the politics of the day. It over-turns the fixed way of things. Here, there is no hierarchy. The first becomes last. The self-effacing are elevated. The ill-bred receive honour. Advance is achieved through giving away. Present security is gained at the expense of future tomorrows. For Jesus, it is a liberation firmly rooted in a relationship with the God he named as Father.

Both make sense only if we understand this liberation against the already-existing commitment on God's part towards his creation. It is a way of living that is rooted in God as expressed through his Messiah. Only when we understand Jesus against this wider Jewish horizon can his own aims be seen and grasped. His miracles make sense: the kingdom is one of generosity and care. His words become weighty and pregnant with resolution: the kingdom is set against all forms of false security, even religion. His actions become windows into the character of the God whose kingdom he announced and whose politics he practised: the kingdom is oriented towards those who have been rejected and ousted by state and religion.

This is the identity of the Christ, the hallmark of the Messiah. It *is* royal: he comes as the LORD's represen- tative. He is agent for the King of kings. But it is neither aggressive nor imperialistic. His empire is made of an altogether different stuff. It *is* priestly: his words and actions will bring new insight into the Law. He will act on his people's behalf and restore their position. But it will be neither military nor mercenary.

Why the big secret?

This helps explain why Jesus never went around saying, 'I am the Messiah'. Had he done so he would only have been playing into the half-baked expectations and hopes of the day. Consequently, he held back from any overt public claim. The nearest we ever get to it is when Peter proclaimed Jesus to be the Christ at Caesarea Philippi (Matt. 16:16; Mk. 8:29; Lk 9:20). Yet even here the popular expectation has moulded Peter's view of Jesus. Peter has in mind the popular view of a divinely anointed, supernaturally gifted king-figure, like David. This king would destroy the contemporary evil political structures and usher in God's kingdom – that is – make Israel the ruling nation once again!

Only Jesus' devastating and withering reply reveals how far off the mark Peter was in his presuppositions. What we can say about this incident is that Jesus accepted the role of Messiah from Peter but refused to proclaim it publicly because of the political overtones that were attached to it.

Indeed, we could go as far as to say that Jesus' death by crucifixion reveals just how much he failed the popular messianic expectations. This is seen clearly in the way in which Jesus was so quickly dismissed by the common people. He failed to meet their spoken and

unspoken expectations. Hell hath no fury like a nation's failed expectations! It is also seen, more subtly, in the way the religious authorities reacted to Jesus. His religious counterparts recognized quite clearly the tone of confrontation in both Jesus' words

and actions. No one takes on the Temple authorities as Jesus did and expects to get away with it. His clearing of the Temple was a declaration of war backed up by consistent haranguing via parable and sermon. That Jesus would die was probably foreseeable. That his death would be the turning point of an altogether new understanding of Messiah – was not.

However, before we go on to explore this in more detail, let's pull things together at this point.

Summary

Thus far we have looked at the different ways in which Jesus understood himself. They can be summarized as follows:

- He clearly spoke into an already existing view of things. It was the story of God and Israel, of promise and unfulfilled expectation. This was the backdrop against which any Messiah talk operated. Expectation was high. Some thought John the Baptist was the Messiah, but he denied it (Jn. 1:15).

- He clearly believed that he had a mission. He reveals this in attributing the Isaiah text to himself.

- He clearly understood the identity of this mission. He reveals this in the way he took God's agenda to those whom established religion and protocol dismissed.

- He clearly understood the risk in identifying himself with the Messiah-figure. He reveals this in refusing to take to himself populist interpretations and expectations or allow the crowds to fulfil their expectations after he performed a miracle (Jn 6:14–15; 7:31).

- He clearly understood the difference between telling the conventional storyline of his hearers and undermining it with his own insights and hopes. This is a recurring theme in his parables (e.g., Mark 12:1–12).

- He clearly understood the cost in assuming his non-conformist messianic expressions. His death is intimately tied up with his messianic identity. Jesus predicts his own death immediately after Peter's confession of him as the Christ (Mk. 8:31–38). At his trial he is accused of claiming to be the Messiah, a charge that appears to constitute the basis of his arrest (Matt. 26:63).

- He clearly expected to be vindicated. His resurrection suggests that his messianic claims were valid, albeit totally unconventional.

Jesus, the Messiah and the first Christians

The meaning of Jesus as Messiah, Jesus as the Christ, is largely hidden in the Gospels. This is largely due to the fact that it could have been misinterpreted. This is not the case, however, when we turn to the first generation Christians. Something very significant occurs. Their understanding of Jesus takes on a clear shape. Indeed, we need just look at Peter's speech soon after Jesus' death to see this (Acts 2:36).

> "Therefore let all Israel be assured of this: God has made this Jesus, whom you crucified, both Lord and Christ."

At a very early stage, then, we have an affirmation of Jesus as Messiah. Unfortunately, we today have lost the full impact of this declaration. To the first hearers this declaration of belief was an affront. There are two causes of scandal. **Firstly,** Jesus is declared Lord. To citizens of the Empire there was only one Lord – Caesar. You do not get any higher than being 'Lord'.

Any Roman citizen listening to Peter on that day would be rightly excused for thinking him to be mad for saying such a thing. The notion of the 'top position' going to someone who had been *crucified* was absolutely insane. **Secondly**, the same can be said for any Jewish listeners. The idea of a *crucified* messiah was so preposterous as to be dismissed out of hand. For both Roman and Jew crucifixion was *the* most abhorrent form of death known in the world. Indeed it was so bad that it was never spoken about in polite company. Therefore, the idea of a *ruler* or *saviour* who was crucified would immediately cause a scandal.

From the start, then, there is immense tension involved in positing 'Jesus' (who was crucified) with 'Christ'. It is a tension, however, that cannot be ignored or abolished. We need to remember that Jesus *Christ* is Jesus the *Messiah*. He is the one whose own story completes the older story of Israel. He is the long-hoped-for-one who would establish the kingdom of God. Crucifixion, Jesus, the kingdom and Messiah – they all hang together in *this* Christ.

Death *and* resurrection serve as the key to unlocking the identity of Jesus. For **PETER**, above, the scandal is overcome by the fact that there is *proof*. It is through *Jesus* that the long-awaited Spirit of God is

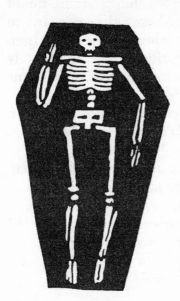

given. Jesus proves his messiahship through giving the Spirit of God to others. The anointed one becomes the anointing one. The one who *received* the Spirit is also the one who *gives* the Spirit. That he was crucified only means that a lot of rethinking has to occur. But note: it takes place within, and is understood by, the older story of God and Israel. For **PAUL**, there is a similar need for reinterpretation. We shall look at this in detail in Chapter 5. Suffice to say, this reinterpretation turns, like Peter's, on the fact of resurrection. If God has really raised Jesus from the dead – that is one thing. But if God has raised from the dead the Jesus who was crucified – then this is an altogether different thing. Its implications, as we shall see, are staggering. It means that some of the most important elements of Paul's belief system have to be reconsidered. The implications for what it means to the older story of Israel are even bigger.

I want to suggest here that two things have happened

The **first** is that the term 'Christ' remains a title. It denotes certain things about the person on whom it is conferred. This would be the case for any person. In this sense, Jesus is no different. In calling him 'The Christ', the first Christians were giving a specific identity to Jesus. They were deliberately ascribing an entire story to Jesus that their fellow Jewish listeners would understand. It evokes the whole identity of Israel. In so doing, it is stating that the hopes and expectations of all the faithful are to be realized in this person, Jesus. To this extent, it is impossible to separate the notion of messiahship from Jesus. According to the first Christians and their stories of Jesus, it is his rightful identity.

The **second** is altogether different. The term 'Christ' is now Jesus' proper name. It acts in the same way that my surname identifies me. I come from a particular nation, country and family.

Each of them marks me out in a specific way. Each makes me what I am. I am the son of a particular family: this influences my identity. I grew up in a particular country: its customs and stories determine how I see much of life. I belong to a particular nation: this impacts how I see myself on the world's stage. As people get to know me, so they discover what makes me *me*. The different influences culminate in my own distinct personality. In some sense, I have the power to determine the meaning of my name. It is no longer a title – it is a descriptor. It is my name.

So with the word 'Christ'. As a **title**, it evokes certain images; it sets specific boundaries; it identifies certain characteristics. Here, the title impacts the person. But as a *name* it belongs uniquely to the one who owns it. Here, the person impacts the title. The person, in this case Jesus, defines the name. 'Messiah' is given a personal identity that belongs solely to Jesus. The term 'Christ' becomes identified with him, with his life, with his particular death. These all impact the title and reinterpret it. They transform an ideal into a reality. And in the case of the crucified Jesus they operate at a deep level. Messiahs are simply not meant to be crucified. Not even in exceptional circumstances are they meant to rise from the dead. Yet these are the hallmarks of Jesus the Messiah. As such, they demand a radical rethink about the identity of the Messiah and the nature of his mission.

Paul best reflects this transformation when he writes to the Christians at Corinth. He talks about the death of Jesus. But note how he refers to Jesus.

> For what I received I passed on to you as of first
> importance: that *Christ* died for our sins according
> to the Scriptures . . .
>
> . . . But if it is preached that *Christ* has been raised
> from the dead, how can some of you say that there
> is no resurrection of the dead? If there is no resur-
> rection of the dead, then not even *Christ* has been
> raised. And if *Christ* has not been raised, our
> preaching is useless and so is your faith . . .
> (1 Cor. 15:3, 12–14)

This passage is one of the earliest passion narratives in
the Christian Bible. It is clear that at an early stage the
title, Messiah, and all its corresponding status of dignity have been attributed to Jesus. Jesus has been
exalted to a very high position.

In conclusion, we can say this. It would appear, then,
that for the early Christians the term 'Christ' was
both a proper name as well as a title of high significance. In a sense, the name 'Jesus' was incorporated
into the title. The one whose life and death is understood to fulfil the story of Israel is recognized in terms
of dignity and authority. Jesus is the Christ. All the
aspects of dignity that belong to the title are now
ascribed to him.

- In calling Jesus the Messiah the early Christians had found a new identity for Jesus – and themselves. It was one which combined both the person called Jesus and the functions expected of the Messiah.

- In reinterpreting the title Christ through attributing it to Jesus the early Christians renamed Jesus against the background of his death, resurrection and his giving of the Spirit at the feast of Pentecost. In doing so, they found the title and ultimate name to be most fitting.

Where do we go from here?

The early Christians were involved in the process of *faith seeking understanding*. They were trying to answer the question, 'Who do you say that I am?' They arrived at a very clear answer very quickly. Jesus is the Messiah. He is the Christ. Jesus is the one who concludes the long story of God and Israel, God and the world. This was to become, in many ways, the dominant understanding of Jesus in the early church.

However, you may have noticed that this is not the only way in which the early church understood the

person, work and significance of Jesus. We are now in
a position to look at other ways in which the Christian
Bible talks about Jesus. We are also now in a position
to say two things about the different ways of talking
about Jesus. **Firstly**, each has to be read against the
wider story of Israel. Outside of this story, their significance is lost and their meaning fudged. To this extent,
then, they must be read in a manner similar to 'Christ'.
Secondly, something has to hold each of these different
angles on Jesus together. If not, we are left with a very
fragmented and disjointed story of Jesus. As one New
Testament scholar puts it:

> **'The multiplicity of christological titles does not
> mean a multiplicity of exclusive "christologies"
> but a glorification of Jesus.'**
>
> M. Hengel, *Between Jesus and Paul* (SCM, London, 1983)
> p.41.

That is, the different expressions used to describe Jesus
within the New Testament do not signify that there is
more than one Jesus. Rather, they provide different
access points, complementary insights into the same
reality. Perhaps it is helpful to remember that the more
complex a reality is, the more need there is for varied
types of expression in order to communicate that reality. So with Jesus.

So –
what are
these
different
ways of
talking
about
Jesus?

We can highlight four that are of particular importance. They are not exhaustive statements about what the early Christians thought about Jesus: there are others even within the New Testament. However, these four are the most important. Thus, they help us in understanding Jesus then *and* now – for each one seeks to throw light on what it means to call Jesus the 'Christ' of God, the Messiah.

They are:

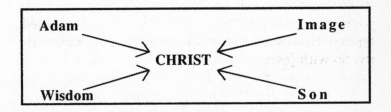

Each of them describes Jesus in a particular way. They are not to be seen, then, in conflict with each other. Rather, each offers a different perspective on the same story. What holds them all together is that they describe something about Jesus, the Christ. They each serve to unpack the true identity of Jesus as the Christ.

Who, then is Jesus? He is the *Christ*.

What kind of Christ is he?

He is what **Adam** should have been:

He is the ultimate **image** of God:

He reveals **Wisdom**:

He is the true **Son** of God.

What we can say is that all these different windows on Jesus hang together on the early church's belief that he is the Christ. To this extent, then, we may call this ultimate name and title a

tensive   symbol.

That is, it does two things. Firstly, it combines all the *tensions* inherent in the story and meaning of Jesus. Whatever Christians believe about Jesus, it is not superficial. It is full of tension. We shall unpack some of this tension in subsequent chapters. Secondly, the name is *symbolic*.

That is, it draws into itself meaning from each of these different access points which, in turn, add to our understanding. Thus, it becomes the location of meaning for Jesus.

Conclusion

- Jesus receives an identity by being called the Christ.

- The meaning of 'Christ' is given significance by being associated with Jesus who was crucified and raised to life.

- 'Christ' is given additional meaning by being associated with other elements of the Jewish story.

- These additional elements, in turn, are transformed and given new meaning through association with Jesus.

- The result is recorded in the stories and writings of the first Christians. They are the beginning of the Christian church's answer to the question, 'Who do you say that I am?'. These are the first responses to the question, 'Why do you believe what you believe about Jesus?'.

5

What Does it Mean to be Human?

Introduction

If we are to take the Old Testament story seriously we must understand one major presupposition of its writers.  It was the belief that human destiny and fulfilment would be fulfilled by the people of Israel. The Bible tells us that it was the people of Israel who were meant to show how humans should live. It would be through **Israel** that all peoples would reach human fulfilment. Therefore, it was to the nation of Israel that the rest of the world should have been able to look in order to see how to conduct itself. Unfortunately, as we have seen, the Jewish nation did not quite live up to this spectacular standard.

It should come as no surprise, however, to discover language within the New Testament that reflects this hope. The first Christians understood this hope to have been fulfilled by Jesus. He is the Christ, the national figure in whom all these expectations have been fulfilled. This is an important point. To miss it is to subvert much of what the New Testament is saying about Jesus. Jesus is fundamentally a *human* figure. The person who would realize and embody all these hopes and expectations would be a man, not a god. Indeed, it was unthinkable that it could be any other way. After all, if the problem was thoroughly human so, too, was the solution.

This, then, leaves modern readers with a double problem. On the one hand, we need to know this older story of anticipation. If we do not we shall miss significant elements to the story and meaning of Jesus. On the other hand, we need to know how and understand why the first Christians expressed their belief that these hopes had been fulfilled. Until we do, we shall miss the full impact of Jesus.

> **We need to know both in order to answer why we believe what we believe about Jesus.**

We have resolved the first problem in our previous chapters. By entering into the Jewish world-view we are more able to understand the world in which Jesus and his first followers lived with all its expectation and hope. As a result we are better informed to see how they understood Jesus to have fulfilled such expectations.

SO HOW DID THE FIRST CHRISTIANS EXPRESS THIS FULFILLED HOPE?

They did so by reinterpreting already existing beliefs and applying them to Jesus.

Earlier we noted that the Jewish belief in a deliverer was a very here-and-now belief. That is, the Messiah would be a very human figure. There never was any belief that this person would be divine. That was the stuff of Roman and Greek – pagan – myths. Consequently, when we turn to the New Testament we see this same emphasis. Jesus is described in fundamentally earthy and human terms.

WHY?

Firstly, because he was a very human figure. His life was very human. His miracles and teaching were very human: Jesus identified the power of his miracles to be that of God's Spirit yet performed by one very much human. And his death was particularly human. His resurrection, too, was very human. In all these stages of life and death Jesus was as human as you and me. Secondly, the purpose of his life, death and resurrection was fundamentally human-directed. Very soon after his death and resurrection people were talking about him as the liberator of men and women.

Therefore, it makes sense that the earliest stories of Jesus described this humanity. Images and concepts were required in order to express the new understanding of Jesus. To do this, the writers turned to their ancient story. In it they found what they were looking for. They found that there already existed theological – and national – ways of expressing this belief. Consequently, they took them and applied them to Jesus. In doing so, a *mutation* in meaning took place. By taking common and popular beliefs and applying them to Jesus the meaning developed, changed, progressed. They did not turn into something they were not before. This would be a sort of complete change in thought. Rather, the original meanings were adapted until they better expressed what the first Christians wanted to say about Jesus.

This was not too difficult a task.

After all, are we not doing this all the time? This is

how language and communication work. In order to describe something new we take something we know and *s-t-r-e-t-c-h* it until it describes what we want to say about something else.

So with the first Christians. They took their already established religious beliefs and s-t-r-e-t-c-h-e-d them to fit what they wanted to say about Jesus.

However, this was no straight parallel. Something profound had happened with Jesus. We could call this the 'Jesus-factor'.

WHEN THE 'JESUS – FACTOR' WAS TRANSFERRED TO THE ORIGINAL BELIEF IT ADDED MEANING, GAVE DEEPER SIGNIFICANCE TO IT.

This combination of the *new* 'Jesus-factor' with already established beliefs enabled the first Christians to communicate more effectively what they believed about Jesus.

This was *faith thinking*.

This was *faith seeking understanding*.

This was how the first Christians came to say *what* they believed about Jesus.

To do so, they first had to know *why* they believed.

• Jesus was raised from the dead.

• Jesus had given the promised end-time Spirit.

Just how would the first Christians communicate such events? These were, after all, mind-expanding thoughts. *No one* had ever thought them possible. Suddenly they were a reality. And they were a reality that had to be expressed, communicated, told. *This* was *good news*. What creative genius could express it? What imagination could communicate what had never before taken place? How would it be possible to talk about it in such a way that people would understand?

ACTIVITY

Write down how *you* think the first Christians arrived at *what* they believed about Jesus. Did it fall out of the sky? Did they make it up? Just *how* did they arrive at what they believed about Jesus?

Hopefully, you will have surprised yourself with your answer. Its truth or falsehood should become clear to you as you read on. What I can assume, though, is that we tend, by and large, to take the end product for granted. Christians today are at the end of the process. As such, an element of familiarity has developed, at best – indifference, at worst. It is a temptation of certain types of Christians to assume that because they think they know what they believe about Jesus it automatically follows that they know why they believe it.

However, I am not so sure this is the case. In fact, it probably is the opposite. Today we can identify the first generation of western Christians who neither really know what they believe let alone why they are supposed to believe it. Rather:

> **everything hangs either on blind tradition (mindlessness), experience (subjectivity), fashion (mass control) or apathy (cynicism).**

As a result, we have lost the true meaning of Jesus, his  life, death and resurrection and giving of the Spirit. Instead of language expanding our understanding it has reduced the meaning of these events. The original storyline has been lost. The words have been set in stone. They have become facts. They are no longer alive, no longer startling, no longer vivid. As a result, they are unable to inspire our hearts and minds and imaginations.

It will become clear, however, that the first Christians had at their disposal religious beliefs that were already well developed. With them they could talk about Jesus as ADAM, IMAGE OF GOD, WISDOM and ultimately, SON OF GOD. We turn now, then, to look at the first two of these terms, Adam and image of God, in order to see what the New Testament writers wanted to say about Jesus.

Part I: Adam

The first Christian thinkers turned to questions about the significance of Jesus and what he achieved. To do this they talked of Jesus as the second Adam. Now the first thing we should ask is, 'Why Adam?'. After all, doesn't he belong to the story of creation: serpents, forbidden fruits and a spare-rib wife? What has he to do with Jesus?

It is at this point that the loss of the Jewish story becomes significant. If Adam is taken out of this story and left to Genesis 1–3 we miss one of the most significant aspects of Jesus' identity. For it is with the figure of Adam that the first Christians were able to unite Jesus with Israel, and through Israel with the whole human race.

WHY?

Well, something very spectacular happened with Jesus. At one level, it *is* spectacular that someone should be
brought back to life. This is,
after all, the kind of stuff
seen in science fiction. So, it
is hardly surprising that
people should ask questions
about Jesus' humanity.
Jesus does appear to be an
extraordinary kind of man.
He died as a human. But he
also came back to life as a
human. Does this mean,
then, that he is some kind of superman?

Fortunately, the New Testament writers do not present Jesus in this way. Why? Because the more ancient
history of the Jews demanded a different interpretation. Sure, had Jesus been born around the time of
Abraham then the notion of a superman might be
valid. But a lot of history had run under the bridge. In
particular, significant development took place just
before the time of Jesus, in what we call the
intertestamental period. Between the close of the Old
Testament and the birth of Jesus, tremendous develop-
ments in religious thought had occurred within Jewish
circles. Remember, the Jewish nation had known
almost complete desolation in its national hopes. Yet,
over time, the hopes remained and grew.

> **AT SUCH TIMES PEOPLE ARE FORCED TO GO BACK TO BASICS.**

For the Jewish people this meant going back to their original story. We considered this in detail when looking at Jesus as the Messiah, the Christ. However, it is important to pick up some aspects of the story again.

- The Jewish God, the LORD God, was the creator of all things.

- He created the first human being, Adam.

- Adam was meant to represent God within his creation.

- Adam failed.

- God chose Abram to be his spokesman, his representative.

- From Abraham came the chosen people.

- The chosen people, the Jews, were meant to be God's representatives.

- As such, they would fulfil God's intention for the whole of the human race.

The basic storyline, then, is that the figure of Adam became a *tensive symbol*. As such, Adam represented – symbolised – everything Israel was meant to be. Israel, it follows, was meant to be the fullest and truest expression of what it meant to be human. Tom Wright puts it well:

> 'Adam language either advances, or develops, a claim about the place of Israel in the purposes of God. It is another way of saying that the world was made for the sake of Israel, or that Israel is God's intended true humanity.'
>
> N.T. Wright, 'Adam in Pauline Christology', *SBL seminar papers*, 1983), pp. 359–389

This is an astounding claim for any nation or religion to make. It smacks of either arrogance, self-delusion or imperialism to the contemporary reader. Yet this is the very stuff of Old Testament and intertestamental religion. If you want an example of true humanity, look at Adam – look at Israel, or at least Israel once God restores it to its true place and glory.

HOW, THEN, SHOULD WE UNDERSTAND JESUS?

The tendency amongst people who have grown up within the church is to think of Jesus as divine. He is God: God walking on the earth. Unfortunately, this is not the storyline of the Gospels. Neither is it the primary storyline of subsequent letters. Jesus is all-too-human. Perhaps the best example of this is in the letter to the Philippians.

Your attitude should be the same as that of Christ Jesus:
Who, being in very nature God,
   did not consider equality with God
      something to be grasped,
but made himself nothing,
   taking the very nature of a servant,
   being made in human likeness.
And being found in appearance as a
   man
      he humbled himself
      and became obedient to death –
      even death on a cross!
Therefore God exalted him to the
      highest place
   and gave him the name that is
      above every name,
that at the name of Jesus every knee
      should bow,
   in heaven and on earth and under
      the earth,
and every tongue confess that Jesus
      Christ is Lord,
   to the glory of God the Father.
(Phil. 2:5–11)

In part of this letter Paul is trying to encourage this socially diverse group of people to get on with each other. To do so, he gives them a contrast. He turns to Jesus. Admittedly, some readers today will have already read this with a divine being in mind. That is, this is the story of a divine being who becomes a human being and then goes back to being divine again. Others, however, will have read it with a human being in mind. Which is correct?

Obviously, the original context will determine a significant part of the original meaning. How would the first hearers of the  letter have understood this passage? How would knowledge of the Jewish story have aided understanding?

In the background of this poem about Jesus lies a more  ancient belief that Israel is God's true humanity. It is true that Adam originally stood for all humanity. In this sense, it is a *backward* looking concept. But by the time of Christ this had been refined. Now, Adam represented Israel in a futuristic sense. Israel is the people of God. As such, God will fulfil his intentions through Israel. It made sense, then, to describe Israel as Adam. Adam represented, then a high future expectation on the part of the Jewish nation. And, just as the  expected future Messiah was a corporate figure embodying the entire nation, so Adam was a *national* and *corporate* figure: not an individual.

This, then, is the background to the passage. This would be playing in the mind of any Jewish Christian believer. In many ways then, the Philippian Christians would have heard this as a double contrast between Adam and Jesus, between Israel (as-God-intended) and Jesus.

First, the writer of Philippians 2 is making a contrast between two forms of existence – between Jesus and Adam – between that of the chosen, obedient people and that of those who are disobedient.

Second, there are two different kinds of responses. One depicts the right response (Jesus), the other the wrong response (Adam, Israel). One is centred in a humanity that is fallen. It derives from a humanity that sought to grasp something God desired to give freely. Adam signifies a humanity that failed the test, as it were. All this is summed up in the figure of Adam. He lost because he was disobedient.

Alternatively, the other signifies a humanity that succeeded because Jesus was obedient. He did not grasp after an exalted position. As a result, even though it led to his death, God bestows on him an even greater position. And it is what Jesus does and how the first Christians related to him that raise further questions about Jesus' identity. These questions will be unpacked in relation to Jesus being called 'Son of God'. Here, however, we want to say that Jesus embodies humanity at its best. His obedience acts as a means of revealing something about God.

WHAT LED THE FIRST CHRISTIANS TO SPEAK OF JESUS AS ADAM?

This passage, then, acts as a window into the way in which Jesus was being understood. It shows that very early on in the church's life Christians realized that his humanity was *very* significant. In turn, this significance only made sense within the story of Israel.

Where is the connection?

There are two significant but very different issues here. There is the **older established story of Israel** and the national identity as Adam. Against this is the **newer story of Jesus**, crucified and raised, the Spirit-giver. If we pull the two together we can see how the early church came to communicate its belief about Jesus. His life, death and resurrection reveal him to embody a humanity that is both new and appears to be the fulfilment of all Israel's hopes.

This is Adam language

They came to understand Jesus in the light of the older story. They took the already established language about Adam and *s-t-r-e-t-c-h-e-d* it to fit their experience of Jesus. The fit was such that the Adam language, in turn, was modified by the story of Jesus. What God intended for Israel – past or future – was now realized

in Jesus. It was no longer appropriate to look to Israel as an example of how humans should live. More, the political and economical rule that typified God's rule – the kingdom of God – could no longer be located with Israel. The new centre was Jesus. What had been traditionally assigned to Israel is now attributed to Jesus. It is Jesus who best embodies God's intentions for creation. Jesus is now the truest expression of what it means to be human.

Making connections

The figure of Adam, then, was the best way of talking about Jesus' impact on and his significance for other human beings. He lived the kind of life expected of us all. Of course, this expression of proper human life was what God originally expected from the nation of Israel. Jesus succeeds 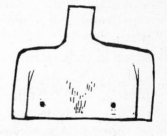 where the religion and nation of Israel failed.

Here, then, we meet one of the most important aspects of what it means to call Jesus the Christ. As the Christ, he is the supreme example of two things. At a **personal**

level his obedience to God's will brings about a new
kind of human existence. As we shall see later, Jesus
initiates a humanity that lives by a different order. He
is the firstborn (Col. 1:15) of a completely new way of
living. As such, he is both the pattern for and the real-
ization of a new kind of humanity. At a **national** level,
he succeeds where the nation of Israel constantly
failed. His obedience shames the historical failure of
Israel. His life, death and resurrection reveal God's
way of doing things – God's glory – in a way expected
of the nation as a whole.

**Adam language suggests there is a kind of
'open-endedness' to Jesus' humanity.**

What do we mean by this?

Well, in many ways the figure of Adam incorporates
both personal and national significance. You will
recall that Jewish believers prior to Jesus understood
the Messiah to be more than a mere individual. The
Messiah was a collective, national identity located in
one person. With the figure of Adam there is a similar
line of thought. Indeed, there may even be a progres-
sion in thought. Adam symbolized a national identity.
Adam was Israel – the true human reality. By attributing the same identity to Jesus the first Christians were
extending Jesus' identity. Jesus was becoming more
than just an individual figure. In this sense, his identity
was becoming *bigger*. At the same time, it was also

becoming less defined by normal human boundaries. Something had happened in and through Jesus that forced the early Christian thinkers to see Jesus in a *collective* sense. It is **Jesus** – not Israel – who is the true Adam both nationally (the new kingdom of God) and personally (as the originator of a new kind of humanity). This was what Israel should have been, but was not. However, with Jesus the politics and economics of the kingdom of God are realized. Therefore, it is Jesus who realizes the human capacity to know God **and** to reveal God through what he does.

In the light of this it was inevitable that Jesus' relation to his fellow humans would come under review. Adam was the recognized answer, because Jesus was doing 'Adam' things.

ADAM LANGUAGE BEST DESCRIBES HOW MEN AND WOMEN SHOULD LIVE BOTH INDIVIDUALLY AND SOCIALLY.

So, we can see that when the first Christian thinkers wanted to express the *humanness* of Jesus, they already had a common language to draw from and use. It

was 'Adam' language. This comes as a surprise to
many people who are conditioned in to thinking about
Jesus in purely 'divine' terms. The notion of a totally
human person does not fit within their understanding
of Jesus. Therefore, for such people, if Adam language
expresses something about the relationship Jesus has
with us as human beings, another question immediately needs to be asked. It is this: where does God fit in?
After all, his death, resurrection and giving of the Spirit
were highly charged events. They demanded answers
both about the kind of man Jesus was and the God who
did these things. Could there be a connection between
the two?

This question makes sense. If the story of Jesus is tied
up with God's intentions for the world, then surely

God's identity must be
conditioned in some way
by the story of Jesus
Christ. Consequently, we
turn now from the ques-
tion, 'What kind of man is
this?' to the more exacting issue of, 'What kind of *God*
are we meeting here?'.

In order for us to answer such questions we need to look
at one particular understanding of Jesus within the New
Testament that acts as a kind of *connection* point. It is
one that expands and develops the humanness of Jesus
in a very important way. It is an appreciation of Jesus as
the one who images God in his humanity.

Part II: Imaging God.

We turn, then, to the whole question of identity. What is the nature of God's identity and how can it be known within creation? In particular, it concerns the identity of the God we come to know in Jesus Christ. What is God's identity? One answer is simply to say, 'Well, Jesus is God'.

If only things were this simple.

However, they are not. Such a response ignores the fundamental distinction the Jewish and Christian Bibles make between God and human beings. They are very different. Therefore, what has to be maintained at all times is the distinction that God is God and human beings are human beings. But this does not mean that there cannot be any point of contact. There is indeed such a meeting point. However, before we look at how the New Testament writers answer this problem let's knock out two *unhelpful* answers that have been put forward as solutions to this problem.

The **FIRST** believes that God and human beings are so different that some kind of mediator has to operate between them. No mediator – no contact. The cult of

saints as mediators between
God and ourselves or the elevation of Mary as mediator have
sought to bridge this gap.
Within this viewpoint it is
believed that prayer to such
intermediaries enables men
and women to make contact with God. Without them
there is no contact, no communication.

The **SECOND** unhelpful answer bridges the gap
between God and humans by making the two almost
the same. That is, the human spirit is over-identified
with God's Spirit. Therefore, they are one and the same
reality. So – if I want to know God, I should get in
touch with the divine within me, with my own 'spirit'.
One consequence of this is the belief that human beings
have instant and immediate access to God. The danger
here is that God becomes an extension of our own
expectations and needs.

Either way, neither response reflects what the first
Christian thinkers thought. Admittedly, for these
thinkers, God is indeed completely 'other' – different –
or what the Bible calls, 'holy'. Indeed, God was considered to be so holy that his name could not be spoken.
Thus, when the Old Testament uses the word 'Lord'
when talking about God, it does so as a substitute term
for God's *real* name, Yahweh.

Yet, this notion of complete difference did not mean
that it was impossible to understand what God was

like. Rather, Jewish believers thought that there was indeed some point of contact between creation and the Creator. And this point of contact is human beings. We see it very clearly in the creation stories of Genesis 1–3. There we read that:

> So God created human beings
>   in his own image,
>   in the image of God
>   he created them;
>   male and female
>   he created them.
> (Gen. 1:27)

Here, then, is the point of contact between God and his creation. Human beings are meant to be the link

between the purely created (creation) and the purely uncreated (God). They are the apex of God's creation. It is almost as if the writers are saying, 'Look, if you want to know what God is like, then look at human beings'. This likeness, in turn, should be seen in both individual human beings and in the way human beings relate with each other. Both dimensions of human existence tell us something about God.

As men and women relate intimately with each other they reflect something about God to the world around. This does not mean that God has two arms and two legs. It is not a physical likeness that the creation story talks about. Rather, by being made *male* and *female* the likeness is **relational**. That is, human beings reflect – image  – represent – reveal – God with the created order by the quality of their own relationships with each other.

But what kind of relationships are we talking about? We can identify three levels of relationship from the creation stories.

FIRSTLY – human beings reflect God in their ability to relate to *God*. In that God is able to relate to himself, so human beings reflect this in their own capacity to relate to God. We see this in the text itself. It tells us that the first humans were able to communicate with God. How else would they know what was expected of them? In turn, the story talks of God walking in the garden seeking out Adam and Eve in order to relate to them. this capacity to relate to God in some form or another, in turn, facilitated the human capacity to reveal God's **glory**. Indeed, as we shall see, to be truly human was to reveal something not only about humanity but also about God. The interesting point to note here, however, is that human beings could do this without necessarily needing to become gods or God.

SECONDLY – human beings reflect God in their capacity to relate to each other. Whatever identity we ascribe to the God of the Jewish and Christian Bibles, we have to account for the difference within humanity. There is male and there is female. *Together* they serve to image God and reveal God's likeness. It does not take too complex a mind to deduce that if this is a reflection of God, then God – *in some way or another* – must be a dynamically *relational* being.

THIRDLY – human beings reflect God in their relation to the rest of creation. The Genesis texts show that human beings are *to rule over* the rest of the creatures. If we turn this round and see it from the other creatures' perspective, then we can see that it suggests that *they* will find their meaning, place, security and blessing in relation to human beings. Human beings, then, are intended, in some way or another, to image God through their **dominion** over the created order. Of course, whilst this word 'dominion' rightly carries negative overtones in today's ecologically aware world, the original text of Genesis uses it in a positive and creative sense. Within their original setting human beings merely showed that they were not *identical to* the rest of creation. They stood in a particular relation to it *as well as to God*.

ACTIVITY

What do you think 'image of God' means? Most of us, probably, have some kind of vague notion of what it might mean. Why not put *your* view down here. *Then,* ask yourself how this is reflected in your understanding of Jesus, if it is at all.

The Genesis creation stories are important for the Jewish and Christian faiths because they contain essential information from the Creator about what it means to be human. You could say that they are the **'manufacturer's handbook'** for the human product! In these stories two important statements are made about the Creator's product – human beings. Human beings are meant to:

1. REVEAL GOD'S GLORY

2. MASTER AND CONTROL THE REST OF CREATION

The significance of this cannot be overlooked. The dignity of human beings is located in our relationship both

to God and to the world in which we live. There is an 'up' and 'out' element to our identity. In terms of 'up' we have significance because we have the capacity to show God to the created world in how we live with God and each other. Being *human* is not an end in itself. Rather, we have meaning *in relation to God and others.* And in terms of 'out', our identity is in relation to the rest of the creation. We are not so independent from the rest of the world as once thought. We are learning that we cannot abuse the earth without conse-

quence. In turn, the rest of creation has a relationship with us that gives it meaning. Creation has a glory of its own which needs to be tended and encouraged, con-

trolled and enhanced by our human involvement. Just think of the difference between woodland that is properly tended and that which is left to itself. One grows well, the other is overgrown. One survives, the other ultimately dies. There is *good* dominion, and there is **BAD** dominion. The creation stories tell us that the manufacturer's intention is the former.

We are now at a point where we can begin to combine what we see about Jesus as the image of God with what we saw when looking at Jesus as the second Adam, the true human-  ity. As we saw previ- ously, Jesus reveals his relationship with God through the things that he did. John's Gospel, in particular, reports the differ- ent 'signs' performed by Jesus. The different signs all serve to show something about Jesus both in his rela- tion to the created order and to God. Let's look at them for a moment.

1. Turning water into wine (2:1–11)

2. Healing an official's son from a distance (4:43–54)

3. Healing an invalid at Bethesda (5:2–9)

4. Feeding a great crowd (6:1–14)

5. Walking on water (6:16–21)

6. Healing the blind man (9:1–7)

7. Raising Lazarus from death (11:1–44)

What can we say about these signs? After all, they are hardly the stuff and matter of ordinary day-to-day human life. In what way can they be seen as validating Jesus as a real *human* being? We can identify a double function to the signs here, in order to help us see the *human* significance of Jesus.

FIRSTLY, THEY TELL US SOMETHING ABOUT GOD'S STYLE OF DOING THINGS.

Jesus is obviously connected with some kind of power to be able to do these things. The question is, 'Whose?'. That Jesus did remarkable things is even seen in the way that the authorities accuse him of being inspired by demonic forces. They assumed that because Jesus was not operating according to the established or expected norms that he must be in cahoots with the arch-deceiver himself (Lk. 11:15). However, there was an alternative view – that Jesus is indeed inaugurating God's kingdom, and that these signs announce that a great renewal was happening. As such, the signs in John encourage or facilitate *faith*:

1:14:   'We have seen his glory . . . and believe;

2:11:   Jesus reveals his glory . . . and the disciples believe;

11:40:   If people believe then they would see the glory of God.

The signs of Jesus, then, give glimpses of God's power. They show that it is with Jesus that God's power is located, where God's presence and action are to be found. Because it is God's power, the signs serve to reveal something about God. They reveal God's glory, God's style of doing things. In so doing, Jesus redefines and fulfils the original manufacturer's intentions.

Jesus –	the new humanity,
	the second Adam
	the true Israel
	the proper image of God
	humanity living according to the
	original design.

WHAT IS SO SIGNIFICANT ABOUT THIS?

It shows that Jesus actually achieves what human beings have both the capacity to do and were originally created to do. He is living out our potential. He does so in such a way so as to also tell us something about God. In this way, Jesus *images* God. It is *Jesus Christ*, then, who is the true image of God.

SECONDLY, THE SIGNS SHOW THAT JESUS HAS CONTROL OVER CREATION.

Each of these signs is a pointer to the fact that Jesus  really is living according to the original handbook, as it were. Within a disordered world *these* actions are the kinds of things that show Jesus to be living out a new kind of life. It is the kind of life that also tells the rest of the world something about God. The fulfilled human also images God. God's power is Jesus' power.

But there is more than this. Most contemporary New
Testament scholars would not admit to the resurrection of Jesus from the dead as being a sign. However,
once we understand the meaning of any sign in the context of the Genesis story we are then enabled to see the
tremendous implication of the resurrection. The resurrection shows that Jesus – the new humanity – has total
control over creation. In what way? Well, if you think
about it, death is the worst that creation can throw at
us. The Jewish and Christian Bibles put this down to
our alienation and independence from God. Death,
then, is the end of life because we are no longer in touch
with the power source that gives us life. Death controls
us. What, then, is the significance of the liberation of
Jesus from death? It is this:

> **The annihilation of the death process in
> Jesus' own body shows that he has total
> power over creation.**

What does this all mean in practice for our
understanding of Jesus Christ?

It is this:

The gulf between God and creation has been bridged in
Jesus Christ. As the image of God, Jesus makes com-
munication between God and creation possible.
Where the first Adam (a collective humanity) failed
Jesus succeeds. The separation between God and the

world is now bridged, albeit in the most unusual and unexpected manner. We no longer need to feel lost, alienated, lonely, separated from each other and from God. Jesus Christ crosses the gap and enables communication. The power at work in Jesus is God's power. Jesus' glory is God's glory. All the signs point to this – that Jesus acts and stands in for God and shows this in the kinds of things that he does.

It should come as no surprise, then, that when we turn to other New Testament writings this understanding of Jesus tumbles out at the highest points of imagination and writing. Perhaps one of the most explicit is to be found in Colossians 1:15–21.

Here, theological atom bombs are being dropped in every line! Adam language, Israel language and image of God language are being pulled together along with wisdom language (which we shall look at next) in order to say something about Jesus' relationship both to God and to the whole of creation. And again, if he really is fulfilling the maker's handbook, this is the kind of evidence that Jewish believers would expect of their Messiah. The scandal comes not in that what was expected actually comes into being. Rather, it is because it happens through the *crucified Jesus*.

He is the image of the invisible God, the firstborn
over all creation;
For in him were created all things in heaven and on
earth
(visible and invisible, whether thrones or
dominions or principalities or authorities);
all things were created through him and to him.
He is before all things,
and in him all things hold together.
And he is the head of the body (the church).

He is the beginning, the firstborn from the dead,
in order that in all things he might be pre-eminent
For in him God in all his fullness was pleased to
dwell,
And through him to reconcile all things to him,
making peace (through the blood of his cross)
through him,
Whether things on earth or things in heaven.
(Col. 1:15–20, RSV)

The gulf between   God

                     and

                     creation is bridged

Here is one of the highest points in New Testament
thinking. It is the high place between creation and
heaven. Here is the resolution of a fundamental
problem in the Hellenistic world at the time of the early

church: how are the two linked? What connects heaven and creation? It might strike us as strange, but the Hellenistic world at the time of Jesus and the early church did not think primarily in terms of sin and its solution. Rather, for the Hellenistic world the *real* issue was that of **SEPARATION**. It was about *feeling lost* rather than *being wrong*, about how we can be united with the Creator, with God. Men and women felt like *aliens* they felt *homeless* and they were *insecure* in their world because they sensed and experienced distance from the Creator.

The amazing point being made in Colossians is the fact that it is Jesus Christ who bridges the gulf of our separation from God and enables union with God.

Jesus Christ gives identity in a world where people are unsure of their place. He is now the supreme centre and location of God's creative and loving activity within creation. And as the text points out, the power that creates is the same power that recreates. Jesus Christ is now the ruler of creation who unites it with God. What is interesting is that the 'image' language includes other insights about Jesus Christ. A major one is the way in which Jesus Christ is described as the 'firstborn' over all creation. In calling Jesus 'firstborn' the writer is telling us that this new humanity, this second Adam, is the one to whom God gives his all. Jesus Christ, not Israel, is now heir to all of God's blessings. And it is those who are 'in Christ' rather than 'in Israel' who will receive the inheritance promised at the beginning of  the story between God and Abraham. For those who have not picked up the nuance here – this is explicit 'son' language. *Jesus* is God's true son, not Israel, and he shows it in his obedience to the Father's will. Just what kind of 'son'– this second Adam – this one who perfectly reflects God – is, we shall have to wait and see.

What we can say, however, is that it is in Jesus Christ that the new humanity finds its true identity. It also means that the unique claim of Judaism to being the place where the creator is at work has itself to be readjusted. God is now to be located with those who identify with Jesus the Messiah. Just look at Romans 8:29

> For those God foreknew he also predestined to be conformed to the likeness of his Son, that he might be the firstborn among many brothers and sisters.

One modern writer describes the apostle Paul's intentions in using such language in this way:

'(Paul) saw Christ as the "image of God" as the risen embodiment of God's plan from the beginning to share his glory with the man he had created. And he under stood this glorious vindication as a reversal of the curse of Deut. 21.23 and therefore as implying God's covenant concern to embrace both outsider and insider, sinner as well as blameless, Gentile as well as Jew.'

J.D.G. Dunn, 'A Light to the Gentiles', in *The Glory of Christ in the New Testament*, (ed. L.D. Hurst, N.T. Wright; Oxford: Clarendon Press, 1987), pp. 251–266.

That is, the benefits that the rest of the world were meant to receive from Israel are now to be found in Jesus Christ. The national, sexual, social, political, religious and economic lines have been shifted – radically. Where the first humanity was exclusive, the new humanity is to be inclusive. The glory of God in Jesus is available for *all* humans irrespective of class, race, religion or gender. To be made in *this* image is to be incorporated into a new and radically different humanity. It is to be connected to and exist within the resurrected life of Jesus Christ, the true human, the one who fully images God.

The New Testament writers are at pains to show that the huge issue of **SEPARATION** has been resolved. Jesus Christ is now the head of the cosmos. The good news is that Jesus removes the barriers that cause separation in the first place (he is the true Adam). Yet he does so in such a way as to show

that there is an intimate relationship between: God, Jesus Christ and the church. Christ may well be the head of the cosmos, but he exercises such lordship within his 'body', the church. This is quite a radical concept – not only is **Jesus** the true Adam, but it is the **church** that should represent the true Israel. Consequently, it is within the church that this intimate union of head and body, God and creation, takes place.

WHY?

Because it is only in Jesus Christ that we can see the creative love of God at work within his world, albeit in a very disarming and challenging manner. However, in order for us to understand **WHAT** this means both in the life of Jesus Christ as well as for the church, we need to turn to another way of talking about Jesus as the Christ.

6

Jesus as the Cosmic Presence of God

Introduction

How we respond at times of crisis gives one of the biggest clues as to our *real* view of life – what we really think about life, death and the universe. In the good times it is very easy to say we believe something about the ultimate meaning of life and death. By and large, our religious beliefs do not get  challenged in times of stability and contentment. Why? Because for most people such religious beliefs are the emergency apparatus of their world-view. They are their 'religious lifeboats'.

HOWEVER...

Once things start going wrong, or expectations are failed, or the goodies dry up, then we are forced to fall back on our emergency plans. After all, that's what they are there for: they are only there for the bad times.

At least, this is one way of looking at such beliefs. Inevitably, if this is how our belief system works then there will always be a gulf between what we say we believe and how we live. Either way, we would have to admit that this is not the best or even the most whole-some relationship between belief and lifestyle. Yet, it would be true to say that even a cursory reading of the Jewish and Christian Bibles shows this relationship to be all too often the norm for Christians in the west today. More importantly, is this true for us today?

ACTIVITY

How you respond to problems tells lots about you. So this exercise is to help you discover this for yourself. What is your immediate response when you suddenly face a crisis that you cannot avoid? Do you try to find ways around the problem? Do you face it head on? Do you deny its existence? Do *you* control it? Or do you let *it* control you?

Hopefully, this task will highlight whether or not we live out what we believe. In addition, it will reveal the extent to which our religious beliefs are mere contingency plans for rainy days rather than expressions of the very way we live and relate to God, each other and the world around us. However, aren't we being a bit idealistic in expecting our religious beliefs to determine how we live in a non-religious culture?

We can reply with one of two positive responses. Both assume that we are indeed meant to live out our religious beliefs in every area of our lives. Both also presuppose that our religious beliefs should inform our lifestyle expressions, our ethics, our business practices, our family relationships – whether or not we live in a Christian society. Where they differ is in the practise of the belief.

The **FIRST** response says this. Our religious beliefs should inform every aspect of life like a set of rules.

 Security is found in what we *do*. Thus, the rules act as a code of conduct in which the regulations of 'the club' are set out. Adhere to the rules, stay within the regulations and you are OK with God. Under such a view, the good people know who they are. They are the ones who keep the rules. They are the 'in-crowd'. It follows that it is very easy to spot the ones who are not 'in'. They do not keep the rules.

Their conduct debars them from membership. The regulations exclude them.

The **SECOND** response says this. Our religious beliefs should indeed inform the way in which we live. However, they do not act as rules which, if followed exactly, admit membership. Rather, they act as *signs*. That is, they signify a particular kind of relationship. So, if we are in this particular relationship with God these are the kinds of behaviour patterns that will be evident. The religious beliefs, then, are not so much something we *do* or *put on* but actually something we *are*. As such, it will be virtually impossible for them *not* to be part of our everyday life. It also follows, if the relationship is a liberating and positive one, that such behaviour will be the expression of freedom and growth.

With these two alternatives we are presented with the stark reality that religion can be both a liberating and a gagging experience. What needs to be said here is that it is not necessarily our following Jesus Christ that is the problem. Rather, as we saw with Peter's confession, it can be that our interpretation of *how-we-do-it* is wrong. If you are having trouble with this idea, why not engage with the following activity:

> Delete each statement with which you do not agree
>
> **The Rules of God are the beginning of wisdom**
>
> **The Regulations of God are the beginning of wisdom**
>
> **Relationship with God is the beginning of wisdom**

If you think about it, there are big differences between rules and relationships. But that is not to say that they are mutually exclusive. Rather, we need to get the order of priority correct. For example, **it is possible** to be obedient to someone with whom you have no personal relationship. By keeping the rules you simply pre-empt any need for the person to relate to you. Whilst your behaviour is good there is no need to have any contact. It is only bad behaviour that necessitates contact. A very good example of this would be the way in which we relate to the police, traffic wardens, judges, dentists! If you think about it, these are hardly examples of dynamic and meaningful relationships.

On the other hand, **it is not possible** to have a deep and meaningful relationship with someone without there being some signs pointing to that relationship. There will be patterns of behaviour, expressions of conduct, fundamental characteristics that reflect a prior relationship. They are only there because of the relationship. If there were no relationship they would not exist. In addition, if the relationship ceased these signs would expire. They would become meaningless.

WHAT HAS THIS TO DO WITH JESUS CHRIST?

Let's summarize what we have discovered thus far in order to see how what we have just read relates to our understanding of Jesus Christ.

- The creation story reminds us that human beings were created:
    - to find ultimate meaning in relationship with God;
    - to reveal God to the wider created world.

- The creation story reminds us that:
    - human beings now relate to God in a dysfunctional manner;
    - God's original purpose for human beings has been blocked.

- The creation of Israel was primarily to re-establish God's original creation-intentions:
    - Israel, therefore, was intended to act as God's image –
    - as God's representative – to the rest of the world.

- The story of Israel reveals that the nation followed the same fate as Adam:
    - Israel related to God in a dysfunctional manner.

- The idea of God not ultimately fulfilling the mandate was unthinkable:

  the figure of Adam became a symbol for the true Israel;

  the people who truly lived according to God's political and economic order would be the long-intended image of God;

- The Messiah – the Christ-figure – would be the one in whom all this failed expectation would be fulfilled.

- The first Christians understood Jesus to be this figure:

  the death and resurrection endorse Jesus as God's true ambassador;

  Jesus is now God's true image;

  if we want to know what God is like then we need to look to Jesus – not the first Adam, not the nation of Israel.

The question, then, to be asked is this:

 How would people know that Jesus was this Christ-figure?

As we saw in Chapter one, Jesus answers this question when approached by John's disciples. Jesus pointed to his actions as evidence of his identity. They showed that God's power was operating. Only someone with God's authority could do them. They must be 'God-actions'. Peter, in turn, points to the resurrection of Jesus and his ability to send the Spirit as evidence of the true identity of Jesus (Acts 2:14–36).

Christian thinkers tend to stop at this point. However, we cannot let things rest here. As we have noted earlier, such activity acts like a sign. It is not an end in itself, as if to say, 'Ah, well, there you are. End of story!'. No – the sign points to something beyond itself. A further question has to be asked, therefore. It is a much more basic and fundamental one. It is this:

How can we know that a person's actions are indeed God-actions?

Admittedly, if these actions are not normal human actions then it is possible that they could be from an evil source. Just what confirms their God-origin?

To answer this, we must turn to another aspect of Jewish belief. It is one that unites both their understanding of creation and salvation (re-creation). It is a more universal and cosmic part of their religious belief. It is the whole notion of **WISDOM**.

Jesus as the Wisdom of God

Whatever you think about Jesus, it is impossible not to admit the genius of his teaching. His collection of sermons and parables stand amongst the greatest ever

spoken by a human. They betray a perception of
human behaviour that is astounding.
Some of his sayings and parables
must have taken the breath out of the
first listeners. Others must have been
utterly enraged. His wit must have
had his audiences laughing for hours
after the telling. There is no getting
away from the pure genius of Jesus.
He understood his culture in a way
most modern sociologists would
covet. He understood his religion in a
way that let ordinary people know
that he was on their side and under-
stood their world. Something about Jesus demanded a
response. In this context we might indeed be correct,
then, to describe Jesus as a **wise man**. But is this what
the New Testament stories do?

It would appear not. The New Testament writers do
not go out of their way to present Jesus as a wise man,
philosopher, sage or guru. They did not need to. A
language already existed that enabled them to talk of
God's action and presence. It was this language that, in
turn, enabled the New Testament writers to begin to
unpack the wider meaning of Jesus. It was 'wisdom'
language. And in order to find out what it means in
relation to Jesus, we need, first, to ask the question:

WHAT IS THE PURPOSE OF WISDOM LANGUAGE?

Put bluntly, it was to do two things. **FIRSTLY**, *such language enabled Old Testament believers to say something about the world God had created.* The

world was made by a wise God. It is not the product of chaos. It has meaning. It is here for a purpose. Despite all the trauma of climate, crop failure and human suffering, creation is ultimately *good*. Wisdom language allowed for such belief. It affirmed that a wise – not chaotic or irrational – God is behind all that is. We see this best in the book of Proverbs, where wisdom is described almost in human terms. Wisdom is described as issuing the threat of judgement in Proverbs 1:20–33. Wisdom stands at the places where people meet and warns them of what will happen if they do not pay heed to her instructions. More positively, wisdom is described as the bearer of good things to all those who take the time to search. Thus, in Proverbs 3:13–18 we read:

> Blessed are those who find wisdom,
>   those who gain understanding,
> for she is more profitable than silver
>   and yields better returns than gold.
> She is more precious than rubies;
>   nothing you desire can compare with her.
> Long life is in her right hand;
>   in her left hand are riches and honour.

> Her ways are pleasant ways,
>   and all her paths are peace.
> She is a tree of life to those who embrace her;
>   those who lay hold of her will be blessed.

But things do not stop here. In Proverbs 8:1–9:1 wisdom is described as having a *cosmic* function. Any crisis over the identity of the created order is resolved in relation to God's *wisdom*.

> The LORD brought me forth as the
>   first of his works,
>   before his deeds of old;
> I was appointed from eternity,
>   from the beginning, before the
>   world began. (8:22–23)

The role of wisdom language, then, is important.

It tells us something about the way the world in which we live was made.

It affirms the goodness of creation. Here wisdom is personified as a personal being: a female figure, the very architect of creation. Such expressions allay any fear that there is no established order to the way the world works. And the good news in this is that, despite the evidence, we are not at the mercy of chaos.

SECONDLY, *it tells us something about the re-created state, about what it means to be saved.* We can identify three major issues here.

- The life lived according to the maker's handbook is one that lives in accordance with God's wisdom. It is to wisdom that human beings are to go if they want to know how to live correctly. Why? Because this is the way they were meant to live in the first place.

 It is little surprise, then, to find that wisdom and Torah are very closely linked in Jewish thinking. Wisdom can be found in the Jewish Scriptures. Therefore, even in times of national crisis, even when the nation of Israel had been scattered and the Temple ruined, it was still possible to talk about knowing God. God could be known through his wisdom. And his wisdom was to be found in the Torah.

- Wisdom was a means of describing how God can be God without being confused with his creation. It also enables us to talk about God's action and accessibility whilst maintaining the difference between God and creation. As such, wisdom language is another kind of *agency* language. Wisdom

GOD

w
i
s
d
o
m

CREATION

is another **agent** acting on God's behalf. As one writer puts it:

> **Wisdom, like the ... Spirit of Yahweh, was a way of asserting God's nearness, his involvement with this world, his concern for his people. All these words provided expressions of God's immanence, his active concern in creation, revelation and redemption, while at the same time protecting his holy transcendence and wholly otherness.**
>
> J.D.G. Dunn, *Christology in the Making*, (London: SCM Press 2nd edn, 1989), p. 176

• Since wisdom is involved in both creation and re-creation the latter cannot contradict or undermine  the former. That is, to be *re-created* is to **fulfil** the original purpose for being created. The new creation neither obliterates the first creation nor replaces the old creation completely. To be saved means a return to the original creation – not to something else. Salvation is about one's *creatureliness*. As such, any philosophy or religious belief which pits the body against the spirit or says that creation is bad but re-creation is good does not belong to the Jewish-Christian stories. Why? Because it fails to take seriously the fact that what God both creates and re-creates is good. It also fails to realize that God creates and re-creates in the same manner.

WHAT, THEN, CAN WE SAY ABOUT WISDOM

- The vast majority of references to wisdom in the Old Testament refer to spiritual understanding, intelligence, insight, knowledge or skill which God gives men and women (Ex. 35:30–35; 1 Kgs.4:29–34; Ps. 51:6; Prov.2:5; Dan.1:17).

- On the other hand, this is no mere wisdom. It is more than knowledge: it is what people need in order to life a godly life Dt. 4:4f; Ps. 37:30f). Wisdom appears to be with God from the beginning, and shares his thought. It is the agent of creation. Wisdom seeks men and women out and makes personal claims on and promises to them. Yet, wisdom is also the agent of judgement.

WHAT DOES THIS MEAN FOR OUR UNDERSTANDING OF JESUS CHRIST?

If we can show that Jesus identifies himself with the figure of wisdom, then two things can be said. **Firstly,** there is clear evidence that Jesus is aligning himself to one of the most central elements of the Jewish story. If he is doing this, then we can assume that Jesus is making stark claims for himself which his contemporaries would not have missed. The figure of wisdom, as we have seen, acted almost like a controlling mechanism for the whole of Jewish expectation and hope. Obviously, then, if God were to act through someone it would be in ways that are identifiable with the way in which he previously acted through and in wisdom. It follows, then, that the one acting on God's behalf would have to have some kind of relationship with wisdom. What we need to ask, here, is this: did Jesus have such a self-understanding? The clearest indication is that he did so and that he very much entertained such a claim. We see this in Matthew 11:28–30 where Jesus says:

> Come to me, all you who are weary and burdened, and I will give you rest. Take my yoke upon you and learn from me, for I am gentle and humble in heart, and you will find rest for your souls. For my yoke is easy and my burden is light.

The significance of this cryptic message is lost on modern ears. We are unfamiliar with Jewish inter-testamental literature. But here, Jesus is lifting a passage from Ben Sirach (also known as Ecclesiasticus) 51:23ff. In this passage wisdom is recorded as uttering the same words. Obviously, then, Jesus is identifying himself, in one fell swoop, with God's wisdom *and* announcing at the same time that only those who come to him will become the true heirs of God's promises.

But the impact does not stop here. Jesus is not only aligning himself with one of the central figures in the Jewish story. He is also aligning himself with the power and presence associated with that figure. If you remember, wisdom is the agent through whom the Lord God creates all that is. In addition, wisdom is the means by which the believer achieves a proper relationship with God.

This really is cosmic language.

Therefore, when we read statements such as, 'And there is but one Lord, Jesus Christ, through whom all things came and through whom we live' (1 Cor. 8:6), we are talking *cosmic* language. Here we confront talk about the cosmic presence and power of God being located – not in wisdom anymore – but in Jesus Christ. It is Jesus – not wisdom – who is the action of God. It is Jesus – not wisdom – who now describes the creative and re-creative energy and character of God. Everything that Jewish believers understood wisdom to accomplish and do, the early Christians now understood to happen and occur in and through Jesus Christ. The life, death, resurrection and ascension of Jesus, as well as his sending of the Holy Spirit, now show that *Jesus* is the creative power of God.

> **Christ . . . is to be understood as the cosmic presence of God: that is to say, the action and manifestation of God which in one sense is inescapable throughout the cosmos has been focused in the man Jesus, or better in the whole 'Christ-event' . . . Christ embodied . . . God's creative energy in as complete a way as it is possible for the cosmos to perceive; which also means that Christ now is to be seen as the definition and norm by which that divine presence and energy can be recognised.**
>
> J.D.G. Dunn, *Christology in the Making*, p.193

However, before we can go any further we need to ask another question. It is this:

WHY DID THE FIRST CHRISTIANS LINK JESUS WITH WISDOM?

You will remember that one of the major stumbling blocks for Jewish believers in accepting Jesus to be the Messiah was the brutal fact that Jesus had been crucified. As all good Jews would know, anyone crucified was cursed under the Law. Deuteronomy 21:22–23 says that,

> If anyone guilty of a capital offence is put to death and the body is hung on a tree, you must not leave the body on the tree overnight. Be sure to bury it that same day, because *anyone who is hung on a tree is under God's curse.*

We tend to miss the significance of this fact. As far as Jewish believers around the time of Jesus were con-

cerned (and today), his death on a cross (wood, tree) meant that he *could not* possibly be the Messiah. Messiahs upheld the Law. They were not condemned by it! Like the Law, the Messiah would save his people. It was inconceivable, then, that the saviour (Messiah) should be cursed by the Law.

However, the fact that God raised Jesus from the dead means that this relationship between Law and Messiah has been turned on its head. By virtue of his resurrection Jesus now stands in a unique relation to the Law. It would appear that it is *Jesus* who stands over the Law, rather than the other way round. Obviously, had Jesus died and remained dead the Law would be seen to be vindicated. That Jesus did not remain dead means that the place of the Law is irrevocably changed. It is now Jesus, not the Law, that best displays God's intentions and purposes.

ACTIVITY

Why do you think Jesus was raised from the dead? Was it because he was God? Or was it because he lived in perfect obedience to God's will? Or both?

The first Christians answered this in relation to *wisdom*. They did so because they understood the profound issues at stake here. On the one hand, not only had they to explain the significance of the resurrection but, on the other, they had to show that in raising Jesus from the dead **God's character remained consistent**. After all, if the Law could change, so then could God. That Jesus was indeed raised from the dead was not a point of debate. The first Christians had seen it with their own eyes. Therefore, they were forced to work through this real problem.

One important event enables us to see how they overcame the problem. It centres around Paul's conversion. On the way to Damascus Paul encountered a strange bright light that flashed all around him. Whilst it is a very dangerous exercise to guess what might be going on in a person's mind, it is a valid exercise to ask just what might have gone on in Paul's mind at this time. The text tells us (Acts 9:1–19) that a conversation took

place between Paul and this bright light. Obviously the light was *personal* in some way or another. It could talk. There is good reason to believe that Paul may well have already had a good idea whose voice this was. The Wisdom of Solomon 7:26 tells us that wisdom is 'the brightness that streams from everlasting light, the flawless mirror of the active power of God and the image of his goodness'. That is, if you wanted to know what God was like, the best description would probably be in the form of a brilliant and shining light. Consequently, if wisdom at the time of Paul was described as an intense light and Paul met a bright light, then it would not be too improper of him to assume that he had won the religious lottery and was the lucky man to whom wisdom had decided to reveal herself. Therefore, when the 'light' informed Paul that it was Jesus whom he was persecuting, at least two things must have happened in his mind.

Firstly, he must have been utterly dumbfounded. Evidence? Look at the test. He does not argue with the voice. He accepts the facts immediately. This great light both exists in reality and is identified as the very person whose followers he is trying to exterminate.

Secondly, it meant a radical change in Paul's entire theological belief system. In contemporary language: if Paul were a computer, his entire hard-disc would have crashed at this point. The entire system of belief that he had inherited and applied so vigorously needed to  be reprogrammed. This was a total reinterpretation of what had been expected. If it were true the consequences were profound, with immediate consequences following.

One major consequence was this and it pertains to our inquiry of Jesus as the Wisdom of God:

As a result of his Damascus road experience, Paul understood Jesus of Nazareth to be the completion of the Law. Jesus brings the Law, the Torah – or older Jewish ways of being right before God – to an end. It is now *Jesus* who acts as saviour: not the Law. The Law was no longer the final comment on how we relate to God (Galatians 3:13–14). Rather, the one whose death was judged by the Law to be cursed was now the one who was exalted and enthroned as the one who brings the Law to an end as the means of being right before God. If this is true, then certain things would follow. It meant that it was now proper and valid to predicate all the things that belonged to the Law to Jesus Christ. And remember – one of the major points of the Law or Torah was that it acted as an **access point** to wisdom.

In assuming a role in relation to the Law, Jesus and the first Christians understood him to assume the role of

 wisdom. God's creative and re-creative power is located in Jesus, not the Law. It is *Jesus* who is the true Wisdom of God. Jesus – the Law fulfiller and the Wisdom of God – reveals God and shows humans how to live a proper (therefore saved) life. After all, the Torah, or Law, was simply the embodiment of God's will that showed how we should live. That Jesus is raised from the dead and can appear as Wisdom simply means that it is he – Jesus – who su-

persedes the Law as the mediator of God's revelation and salvation. If this is true, then it means that:

JESUS IS NOW THE TRUE EMBODIMENT OF GOD'S WISDOM.

One scholar summarizes well what must have happened to Paul's 'software' – to his religious and theological beliefs – as a result of this experience.

> He knew ... that Christ had brought the Torah to an end as the embodiment of the divine will and as the means of salvation, that Christ himself superseded it as the true mediator of God's revelation and salvation. This led Paul to reflect upon Christ's relationship with Wisdom. If the Torah was formerly thought of as the embodiment of the divine Wisdom and was indeed identified with her ... it is now Christ who has revealed himself (instead of the Torah) to be the true revelation of God, that is, the true embodiment of the divine Wisdom, indeed Wisdom herself. Thus Paul 'identified' Christ with Wisdom and transferred to him the predicates of Wisdom – pre-existence and mediatorship in creation which were in Rabbinic Judaism transferred to the Torah.
>
> S. Kim, *The Origin of Paul's Gospel*, (Tubingen, 1981), p. 127

As a result of this understanding, the first Christians were able to predicate to Jesus a language that made more sense of what happened in the resurrection and giving of the Spirit. The power that was active in creation and necessary if men, women and entire nations were to live as citizens of the kingdom of God – this power – was now located, centred, fully embodied, expressed, active in **Jesus Christ**.

Once we get our minds around this, our understanding of Jesus goes into hyperspace. This is not the kind of thing that we say of ordinary men and women. Something altogether different is happening here. Jesus has taken on a cosmic identity. In realizing that *Jesus* is the Wisdom of God, the first Christians have been better enabled both to understand and express what God really has done in reconciling the world to himself in Jesus. They present him as God's

chief agent.

And the important point to remember here is this: it is not the notion of a chief agent that was the issue. This was clearly part of the older Jewish tradition. Rather, what was so radical here was that this role was being attributed to a man who had died on a cross.

It was the language of wisdom that enabled the first Christians to talk about Jesus Christ in terms of their Jewish story. It is no longer the Law and observance of the Torah that saves us – it is a relationship with Jesus the Christ. And it was a language that related Jesus to the central figure of this story – the God of Israel who is now ultimately the God of our Lord Jesus Christ.

The question begging to be asked, then, is this:

JUST WHAT IS THE TRUE RELATION OF THIS MAN JESUS THE MESSIAH, THE SECOND ADAM, THE TRUE IMAGE OF GOD AND THE VERY WISDOM OF GOD TO THE GOD OF ISRAEL HIMSELF?

For this we have to turn to the whole question of what it means to call Jesus the 'Son of God' within the New Testament.

Jesus as the Son of God

Thus far we have looked at the different ways in which the first Christian thinkers of the New Testament sought to express their belief about Jesus. Jesus tells us what it is to be truly human: Jesus is the true Adam. Jesus also reveals what true obedience to God is like: Jesus is everything Israel was supposed to be. In addition, Jesus is also identified as the true source of power behind the whole of creation: the one who saves is also the one through whom all things came into existence in the first place. In all these ways the different writers are saying something significant about Jesus. And what holds them all together is the fact that much of what they are saying is concerned with Jesus as he relates to creation.

**But what about
Jesus' relationship with God?**

As we saw in the last chapter, it is the cosmic signifi-cance of Jesus that raises questions about Jesus' relationship with God. And this exalted status is expressed in **two** very distinct ways.

FIRSTLY

Jesus is the one through whom all things are made (Col. 1:16ff.). That is: the power at work in creation is the same power now at work in salvation, or 're-creation'. To be *saved* is to be reconfigured with the Creator's original intention for creation. It means to be *realigned* with creation, not made different to it. And as we have seen, this is what it means to identify Jesus in *cosmic* or *creation* terms. Jesus is both the true Adam and the wisdom of God. That is, Jesus not only lives the true human life but actually shares the unique attribute of creating with God.

SECONDLY

Jesus is the one through whom we make contact with God (1 Jn. 2:1). As God's chief agent, Jesus is his ultimate representative. It is *Jesus* – not the Law or the nation of Israel – who represents God to his creation and who represents creation to God. Such a status raises profound questions. And an understanding of such questions is central if we are to identify Jesus properly. Why? Because these questions constitute the very tension that the New Testament writers are trying to resolve. We identified it at the end of the previous chapter. It is this:

The New Testament is quite clear on the answer:

Jesus Christ is God's Son.

However, what does this actually mean?

In order to discover the meaning of this status we need to go back to what we learned in the opening chapters. There we learned that the world of the first Christians was informed by the ancient stories of Israelite faith. We saw, too, that the first-century world had its own view of reality – its *world-views*. More importantly, we learned that it is easy to read **our** world-view back into the Bible. This, perhaps, happens mostly when we come to look at Jesus as the Son of God because when we read the New Testament it is very easy to forget that it was written by people who did not have such a thing as the doctrine of the Trinity. For the first Christians God is One. And yet today we believe God is One yet Three.

In order to let the original texts speak to us, we need to put Christian understanding in its proper chronological order. Therefore, we need to put the horse before the cart. In this case, it means putting what the New Testament writers say first. Only once we have clarified what they have said can we then look at what subsequent Christian thinkers have said to see if it conforms with the original story.

Thus, for the moment we shall
put any later understanding **on
hold**. This does not mean that
we reject it. Quite the opposite:
the doctrine of the Trinity was
developed by later Christian
thinkers in order **to explain** what
is said in the New Testament.

Therefore, we need to identify
the *primary* problem or tension before we get to any
subsequent answers. And the primary problem here
concerns **Jesus and his relation to God**. Therefore, we
need to see just how much the first Christians struggled
with this profound tension and how they resolved it.
That is, we look at *their* faith seeking understanding.
For them it centred around **two** tensions.

- The first concerns how Jesus, rather than the Law or
  the Temple religion, could be the centre of salvation.
  As we have seen, this was resolved by drawing on
  Adam / Wisdom / Image of
  God language. In so doing,
  the first Christian thinkers
  did two things. On the one
  hand they used it as a means
  to describe Jesus. Yet, on the
  other hand, they also used the
  historical reality of Jesus' life, death and resurrection **to redefine** these terms. This was no mere
  straight transference of data from one to another.

Rather, Jesus actually reinterpreted the old concepts. Serious reinventing, re-imagining had to take place. The New Testament writers clearly understood that Jesus added **new meaning** to their faith.

- The second tension concerns how Jesus, rather than Israel, could be the centre of divine agency. And resolving this involves going back to the first Christians' **world-view**. Inevitably, this is a complex matter, so we shall focus on just two or three aspects that are most pertinent to our question. We can summarize them neatly:

- **God is One.**

- **God never makes himself known directly.**

- **God relates to his creation via a *mediator*.**

What is important to note is that the New Testament writers overcome this tension to a significant degree by referring to Jesus as God's Son.

WHY?

FIRSTLY, because the idea of sonship communicates status and authority. The idea of sonship is not uncommon in the Bible. It signifies rank and legal legitimation. Within the *'honour-shame'* cultures of the biblical world, when the head of the family, or business or nation – the 'boss' – could not attend he would send his heir, his son. In this role, the son acted as legal representative. As such he would be given the same honour and dignity as would normally be given his father. It would be as if the father were there himself. Thus, in honouring the son, the host was in fact honouring the father. And in disrespecting the son the host would be directly insulting the father.

We can see, then, that we are dealing with a **relational** characteristic here. Sonship reveals that a person or people has a special relationship with God. And as with any relationship, there are necessary characteristics.:

- Sonship is something conferred by God

- Sonship denotes a special status

- Sonship specifies representation

- Sonship carries with it obligation and commitment.

With this in mind, then, as we turn to the Old Testament, we see that the idea of sonship is applied in a number of different ways. In Malachi 2:10 there is an implicit reference to Adam as a son of God. In 2 Samuel 7:14 the king (in this case the future king, David) is called 'son'. We even see particular Israelites, as well as Israel as a whole, being given this title: Deuteronomy 14:1–2, Jeremiah 3:19–20, Hosea 1:10. And this tradition is extended into the time between the Old and New Testaments, the inter-testamental period, where those who remain righteous before God or charismatic leaders are also referred to as 'sons' of God. Therefore, we can say:

> **At around the time of Jesus, the language of divine sonship was widespread both within Israel and in the wider world.**

In essence, it was used to describe people who acted on God's behalf either to the world at large or to the covenant people in particular.

It is hardly surprising, then, that we should find this same kind of language in the New Testament. In particular, we discover that Jesus uses the title 'Father' some 51 times. This consistent use of the title by Jesus tells us something very loudly and clearly. It is that Jesus understood himself to have a very specific and distant relationship with God. In particular, it reveals that Jesus was aware of God's love for him.

We see the nature of this relationship in the way that Jesus talks of God as his Father. He does so in very

intimate ways. Jesus clearly does not perceive God in any distant or transcendent way. The God of Israel is his 'Father' and he is his 'Son'. And for Jesus this sonship reflects two essential characteristics.

On the one hand, it communicates a sense of intimacy – Jesus relates to *God* the Father in a way that reveals a closeness of relationship. On the other hand, Jesus understands *himself* to have a very specific identity in relation to God: *he* is God's most superior representative. He acts as the son who represents his father. Therefore it follows that to honour Jesus is to honour the God who sends him. To dishonour Jesus, however, is to dishonour the God in whose name, and therefore with whose authority, he comes.

That much is clear – but what does it mean? Does Jesus understand his special relationship to God any differently than we understand ours today? Or does Jesus actually understand himself to  have a special relationship with God that marks him out from everyone else?

In order to answer such questions, we have to look beyond the term 'son'. So – where do we see the evidence of Jesus displaying his identity as son? We can identify four examples. Two are of major consequence and therefore we shall spend a little more time on them than on the first two. However, between them they build up a picture of Jesus that points to only one reasonable answer to the question we are asking with regards to the kind of sonship we meet in Jesus Christ.

I. Sonship and the kingdom of God.

We noted earlier that when Jesus first announced his mission he did so within the context of inaugurating the kingdom of God. Whatever it means to be 'Christ', to be the *true* Adam or Israel, to embody the very Wisdom of God, it is tied up with God's kingdom. And the one who exercises God's authority and presence in such a manner rightly deserves the honour of being called 'Son'.

This proclamation is, in turn, expressed in Jesus' parable of the vineyard keeper that follows (Matt. 20:1–16). As such, it offers us a profound insight into

his own self-consciousness, his own sense of identity. In his story, Jesus identifies himself with the owner's son. It is also clear that Jesus' opponents understood what he was saying. It is clear that God is the owner, Israel is the vineyard, Jesus is the heir and the Pharisees are the rebellious tenants. In essence, Jesus is identifying himself with God on a very intimate level. He is the one who truly represents God. Also – Jesus succeeds where everyone else has failed. Indeed, Jesus identifies himself as the true son who fulfils the obligations and commitments inherent to the relationship of sonship. Where Israel as a nation failed, Jesus succeeds. It is small wonder that he alienated the religious leaders who were so offended.

From the parable it is clear that Jesus *did* understand himself in a way that was consistent with the thinking of his day. We can say that Jesus understood himself as God's final agent or representative. Jesus, then, is on the king's business. Admittedly, Jesus did not come across as a typical representative of God. People expected someone more 'royal' (hence the wise men went to King Herod) or 'priestly' (hence the religious leaders were so mollified by Jesus' claims). However, the gospel writers are clear on this point: it is not Jesus who ought to be ashamed of making such claims. Rather, it should be those who do not honour Jesus' claim, for in so doing they dishonour the God he represented.

 Such examples clearly point to the fact that Jesus' sonship is intimately linked with God's kingdom. Jesus *is* God's son because he is God's true representative: he is the one who takes supreme place in the kingdom of God. Therefore, when sonship is used in this way we see Jesus being described in a similar way to Old Testament kings, such as David (2 Sam. 7:14; Ps. 2:7). Jesus as son thus acts in a manner similar to that of king: he is the absolute representative of God to his people. If you want to know what God is like, what God is up to, then all you have to do is look at and to Jesus Christ.

2. Sonship and miracles.

Another way in which we might assess Jesus' claim to
be God's son is by his ability to perform miracles. After
all, one very practical way of determining this claim is
to ask for proof. But what kind of proof? A further
example of how the New Testament writers answer
this can be seen in the way they understand Jesus'
miracles. For instance, when the religious leaders
questioned Jesus about the legitimacy of performing
miracles he replied, in Luke 11:20, that the miracles
were evidence of God's kingdom. This is certainly the
case, as we saw earlier, when John the Baptist's disciples
came to Jesus asking for 'proof'. In a thoroughly Jewish
manner, Jesus pointed them to his miracles in order to
authenticate the claims of the one performing them.

This same reality was seen at work when Jesus sent his
own disciples out on missions. He empowered them to
perform miracles (Luke 9:1–6). Why? Because if the
kingdom was being proclaimed it had to be backed up
with proof! And since the kingdom is *God's* kingdom,
people should expect to see *God's* actions.

Thus, people expected to see Jesus exercise authority
over all that held them in bondage:

- Illness: he cures the sick (Lk. 7:1–10)

- Hunger: he feeds the hungry (Mt. 14:13ff.)

- Death: he gives life to the dead (Lk. 7:11–17)

- Nature: he controls the elements (Mk. 4:35–41)

Now, of course, we can explain away or *demythologize* such miracles and decide that they did not happen. Admittedly, it follows that we have
no reason or foundation for claim-
ing Jesus to be very different from
ourselves. However, if we allow
the Gospel stories to address us and
challenge *our* world-view, then
something different happens. If we
accept the authenticity of the miracles, we really do have reason to ask
specific questions about Jesus.
(After all, the majority of people
who have ever lived and who are
living now are open to the miraculous: any scepticism is a
relatively modern phenomenon.) So, we must ask, 'Just
what kind of person can do things that scream out
"God"?'. For the first Christian believers it was obvious –
their purpose is to authenticate Jesus' identity as Son of
God so that we might believe in Christ as such (Jn. 20:31).

3. Sonship and resurrection.

However, it is the resurrection of Jesus from the dead
that begins to push out the boundaries of belief. After
all, there have been and probably always will be people
who can do extraordinary things. But not many come
back to life in the way Jesus did.

The Bible describes death as a real event. Death is the
logical and chronological consequence of 'sin' and
signifies our ultimate independence from God. Thus,

'sin' is about a state of *being* rather than the *doing* of specifically *bad* things. After all, if sin is about not *relating* to God in an intimate, dependent manner then it follows that we can do this in any number of different ways. Some people can be explicitly 'bad' but others can be just as 'good' but still as 'sinful'. Jesus describes the religious leaders in the latter category: even 'religion' can separate us from God! As far as the Bible is concerned, anything that keeps us from being dependent upon God is 'sin'.

Thus, each death, as it were, confirms our true state of being when we live apart from relationship with God.

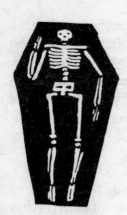

It confirms that to live apart from God who is the source of life ultimately leads to non-life, that is, death. The resurrection of Jesus from the dead, on the other hand, is equally as real an event. It signifies the opposite of death. It shows that Jesus was indeed telling the truth about himself. He really was from God. It also proved that he did speak and act with an absolute authority that came only from God. And only one standing in for God himself could do this. As such, it is entirely proper to call Jesus God's *son* – he does everything a Jewish believer would expect God's son to do.

Paul puts it this way in Romans 1:3–4 when he describes Jesus Christ in terms of what God has done:

> The gospel concerning his Son, who was descended
> from David according to the flesh and designated
> Son of God in power according to the Spirit of holi-
> ness by his resurrection from the dead, Jesus Christ
> our Lord. (RSV)

The resurrection, then, reveals the true identity of
Jesus. Through resurrection God vindicates Jesus' pre-
Easter activity and speech. It is not that the resurrection makes Jesus something he was not before. Rather,
it makes public something that was clear to only a few
prior to his resurrection. As one commentator puts it,
to say that Jesus

> was 'Son of God' was to ... acknowledge him to
> be God's actual representative on earth,
> to whom the same homage and obedience
> would be due as if one were suddenly in the
> presence of God himself ... For the most
> part only heavenly beings or demons would
> have been in a position to draw this
> conclusion ... It was only after his death and
> resurrection to the right hand of God that ...
> Jesus could be acknowledged ... as Son of God.
>
> A.E. Harvey, 'Christ as Agent' in *The Glory of Christ in the
> New Testament*, pp. 248–9.

What was veiled prior to the resurrection is now clear
for all to see. Why? Because prior to the event Jesus
was *proclaiming* the kind of liberation soon to be on

offer for those wanting to participate in God's kingdom. After the event the liberation is actual: and therefore the identity of the one who brings it about is able to be disclosed. Jesus' identity as Son, therefore, is linked intimately with the kind of liberation – salvation – he initiates. It is a liberation *into* his Father's government, the kingdom of God. As the American theologian George Lindbeck reminds us,

---

It is through Jesus' saving work that his personal identity as fully human yet Son of God becomes manifest.

'Atonement' p. 231

Therefore, when we look at what this saving activity involves and how it expresses itself, then the true reason for calling Jesus 'Son of God' begins to emerge. In so doing we can identify the major reasons why the first Christians could so comfortably call Jesus by such an exalted title.

4. Sonship and worship.

Thus far we have been looking at what Jesus has in common with the biblical understanding of sonship. Jesus fulfilled contemporary expectations, albeit in a somewhat unconventional way. However, it is when we turn to what marks Jesus off as

different

that we discover something radical. It has to do with what happened when people met Jesus, or saw what he did, or experienced him in different ways. They saw that when Jesus did all these things he was doing them **GOD'S** way. The Bible uses the word 'glory' to describe this. And what it meant for Jesus was this: he so fully shared in God's glory – in God's way of doing things – that they called Jesus LORD in the same way as they called God 'LORD'.

WHY?

If you have read the first book in this series on the Holy Spirit then you will know that two of the most distinctive facts about Jesus relate to his relationship with God's Spirit (For a more detailed argument than what follows see Chapter 2 of *Why Do You Believe What You Believe about the Holy Spirit* [Carlisle: Paternoster. 1998]).

FIRSTLY, after his resurrection and ascension Jesus exercised authority over the Holy Spirit in a way that paralleled God's own authority. This is an astounding claim. If Jesus is Lord of the Spirit, fundamental questions are raised concerning his relationship to God. After all, the Holy Spirit is *God's* Spirit first and foremostly.

> It was Jesus' relation to the Spirit that forced the
> early Christians to ask about his relation to God.

SECONDLY, the Spirit made Jesus present in the
same way that the Spirit made God present in the Old
Testament. Jesus is not only Lord of the Spirit, he is
also the one whom the Spirit makes real and active
amongst God's people. The Spirit is now ruling for
Jesus and making Jesus present in a manner which
parallels that activity originally performed on behalf of
the Lord God himself.

SO WHAT?

We must remember that the Old Testament presents to
us an understanding of the Spirit as be God's
 *forcefield*. Consequently, 'God-ac-
tions' energized by God's Spirit sig-
nified 'God-presence'. But now, in
Jesus Christ the Spirit makes *Jesus*
present. 'God-actions' energized by
God's Spirit now signify the presence of **JESUS**. So – in Acts 16:7 we
read that Paul was stopped from
going on in his missionary journey to
a particular place by the Spirit. What
is of such interest is the fact that the
Spirit is described now as 'the Spirit
of Jesus'. Jesus is now intimately associated with the
Spirit of God to such a degree that the Holy Spirit is

now identified as being about *Jesus'* business. Jesus'
business – God's business: but the same Spirit. The
implications are far-reaching: Jesus is being described
with attributes identical to those ascribed to God.

This is an innovation of tremendous importance. The
New Testament writers appear **both** to know what
they are doing **and** to be quite comfortable about doing
so! This would suggest that the *divine* identity we
accord to Jesus is not so far off the mark as modern
commentators would make us think. And if we want
further evidence we need only look at the way in which
the early Christians **RELATED** to Jesus. It was this:

THE EARLY CHRISTIANS
WORSHIPPED
JESUS

This is a awesome statement to make. Remember, one
of the fundamental and core tenets of the Jewish faith
is the belief that God is **ONE** and that he alone is
worthy of worship. And yet, when we turn to the New
Testament, we see Jesus being ascribed attributes that
belong solely to God:

- Jesus has authority over the Spirit (Jn. 15:26).

- The Spirit makes Jesus present amongst his followers (Jn. 16:12–15).

- Jesus is the focus of worship (Phil 2:9–11).

Ultimately, the first Christians are unequivocal about their testimony of Jesus. Their actions betray their beliefs about Jesus. He shares an authority equal to that of the Lord God himself.

Thus

- the Lord God who is described as the first and the last, besides whom there is no god (Is. 44:6; Rev 1:8)

is also identified with Jesus,

- the One who died but came back to life (Rev. 1:17; 2:8; 22:13).

!! IMPORTANT POINT !!

> The New Testament Christians use such language to unpack what SON language means when applied to Jesus Christ. They are clearly ascribing 'GOD-IDENTITY' to Jesus Christ. What used to be said only about the Lord God of Israel is now being said about Jesus, his Messiah. Thus – to name God the Father is to name Jesus his Son who is made known through the Spirit.

Conclusion

Perhaps we can draw our conclusions concerning the use of son language in relation to Jesus by pulling together the various threads in two couplets:

A.

On the one hand, we must allow for the fact that there were constraints within Jewish monotheism to which Jesus and the first Christians submitted.

On the other hand, we must allow for the fact that Jesus assumed a unique and God-given authority for what he did.

AND

B.

On the one hand, we can say that **SON** language has to do with Jesus' supremacy of *position* as God's chief agent or representative.

On the other hand, we can say that Jesus' 'authority over the Spirit of God' suggests that his supremacy is to be explained in relation to **GOD** and not merely in contrast with other agents.

In this conscious act of reconfiguration and re-identification, the identity of God is revealed in a radical manner. God now shares his identity with Jesus Christ. This, in turn, challenges the theological 'grammar' of the day. New ways of speaking have to be developed. It is Jesus who shows us the *true* view of God. And he does so by making us privy to different perspectives on the same reality.

This is the reason why the
New Testament writers use
every means possible to
unpack the meaning of God
in Jesus. Through his obedience to the divine will, Jesus
brings about a new kind of
humanity – a radical society

– that can only be described in terms of *God's*
kingdom. And Jesus is the one who brings it about. As
such he is the true Messiah, the Christ of God. In turn,
this 'messiahship' is identified on several levels, each
one describing something about both God and the
Christ. Perhaps the summary below best pulls together
the different levels of understanding of what it means
to call Jesus the **Christ**.

Creator seeking out creation

                so we speak **Adam** language;

Being casting reflection

                so we speak **Image** language;

Sovereign appointing heir

                so we speak **Israel** language;

Father loving

                so we speak **Son** language.

We can see, then, that the identity of Jesus within the New Testament is a complex one. It grows out of,

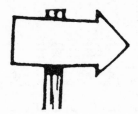 develops and fulfils the more ancient story of Israel. Therefore it is right and proper to expect Jesus to be described in terms that are thoroughly Jewish. In conclusion, then, we can identify three levels of

description – each of which points to specific aspects of Jesus' identity.

1. As the **Christ** Jesus is anointed to inaugurate God's kingdom. Since those who participate in this new social entity constitute a new way of being human it is right to describe the originator of this new species – Jesus – as the new **Adam** and as the **Image of God**.

2. In turn, we see that the means of participation in the new kingdom has changed. It is no longer through keeping the Jewish rules and regulations embodied in the Law. Rather, participation – and therefore *salvation* – comes through obedient relationship with Jesus Christ. It is now through Jesus that we participate in the new kingdom of bad. Therefore, it is right to describe Jesus as the **Wisdom** of God.

3. Lastly, the evidence of Jesus' own obedience as well as God's approval is located in the resurrection of Jesus from death. Jesus really is vindicated as God's supreme representative. More, Jesus' Lordship over the Spirit of God reveals his true identity. He fully shares in the authority, dignity and being of God. Such a relationship necessitates the language of **Son**.

ACTIVITY

We have looked at the various ways in which the New Testament Christians understood Jesus. Each is an attempt to communicate something about him. Perhaps at the end of this book you can look at how your understanding of Jesus has developed – or even changed – by answering these last two questions. Firstly, what surprises you the most about the way in which the first Christians saw Jesus? Secondly, what presentation of Jesus do *you* identify with most?